**We can be heroes
For ever and ever
What d'you say?**
– David Bowie.

For heroes.

**With gratitude & love to Debs, Daniel & Darley,
my beautiful heroes forever
– for patience & love while I wrote this during the
coronavirus lockdown in Spring 2020.**

@DavidHurstUK

Contents

Introduction

or

How chaos captured in a net never makes order

"It was really scary... but then it was beautiful."

That's how my ten-year-old son Daniel described the final part of The Neverending Story fantasy film when I asked what I'd missed after falling asleep towards the end.

I recalled the earlier line in it said by the old gnome lady Urgl: "It has to hurt if it's to heal."

Both sentences can be used to sum up the Hero's Journey and the 12 Steps, the recovery programme or "a design for living" successfully worked through and lived by millions of people since the book Alcoholics Anonymous outlined it when published in 1939. That book gave its name to a growing group that until then had no official name, and that most commonly now is known simply as AA. (Not to be confused with British breakdown service the Automobile Association or American Airlines, although all these AAs are to varying degrees rescuers of stranded people...)

As well as being used by alcoholics to recover and stay recovered from their once hopeless condition – and alcoholics were previously unfathomable to even the greatest medical and psychological minds, and so essentially left to die – it has also been adapted to work the same miracle for many other debilitating, isolating, despairing and fatal conditions and addictions. This includes addiction to such as illegal and prescribed drugs, work, technology, hoarding, sugar, external validation, gambling, relationships, sex, pornography, food, nicotine, emotions, codependency and love.

In fact it can work for any addiction: that is anything that is detrimental to a person and/or anyone around them that the person cannot stop doing – and stay stopped. Anything that is a distraction or that provides pleasure or relief or numbness has the capacity for someone to become addicted to it. There is today even a group called All Addicts Anonymous, which is "AA, as adapted for all addicts and all addictions".

But as well, increasingly, it is seen that these remarkable 12 Steps can help immensely – entirely – anyone suffering from all manner of emotional problems, mental health conditions, sickness or disease.

More people than ever are interested in them and discovering they are modestly yet abundantly a way of living that creates and gives a meaningful and happy life of comfort that's beyond their wildest dreams, that the 12 Steps are a series of only positive measures that anyone can do, and with not a single "don't" in them. It is not a programme of "don'ts," but of "dos."

Indeed, as far back as 1953 with the publication of AA's guidebook to the 12 Steps, Twelve Steps And Twelve Traditions, its Foreword made the observation that: "Many people, nonalcoholics, report that as a result of the practice of AA's Twelve Steps, they have been able to meet other difficulties of life. They think that the Twelve Steps can mean more than sobriety for problem drinkers. They see in them a way to happy and effective living for many, alcoholic or not."

The man who wrote most of that book, one of AA's co-founders who was a New York-based stockbroker called Bill W, had written three years previously: "I don't think happiness or unhappiness is the point. How do we meet the problems we face? How do we best learn from them and transmit what we have learned to others, if they would receive the knowledge?

"In my view, we of this world are pupils in a great school of life. It is intended that we try to grow, and that we try to help our fellow travelers to grow in the kind of love that makes no demands. ... When pain comes we are expected to learn from it willingly, and help others to learn. When happiness comes we accept it as a gift, and thank God for it."

This essential aspect of living well by being capable of meeting the problems life throws up was also made by naturalist, geologist and biologist Charles Darwin in the previous century: "It is not the most intellectual of the species that survives; it is not the strongest that survives; but the species that survives is the one that is able to adapt to and to adjust best to the changing environment in which it finds itself."

That is, we need to be adaptable to change. As author and pastor John C Maxwell says: "Change is inevitable... growth is optional. To grow you must see the value in yourself to add value to yourself and others. You must know yourself to grow yourself, and it is hard to improve when you have no one but yourself to follow."

So imagine, or maybe you don't need to imagine, that you're a million miles away from where you could be. If you are, you more than likely know this. It may be buried deep down, but deep down you know it. You can do something about that. You can go to the place where you could be. More than that, you can go to where you should be, where you're made to be. You can make those changes, those adaptations and adjustments, that you need to make to be that person you were meant to be. Sometimes these are small changes. Sometimes they are like the response to someone I know, who had needed half his stomach removed due to his heavy drinking, who on starting the 12 Steps asked someone around a long time in AA exactly what he needed to change. The reply was: "How about absolutely everything!"

There's a phrase that's popular now that says: "It's okay to not be okay." It should I think say: "It's okay to say or admit I'm not okay." That's what I think it's being used to mean. I hope it's not being used to mean that it's okay to not be okay, always, for all of your life. That is plainly not okay. No one was put on this Earth to be that way. That would be pointless, that would be life without real purpose, maybe that is a life that has not adjusted or adapted or made any changes. Many people come into the 12 Steps groups talking about having the same emotional reactions as when they were a child or a teenager. Okay, there's some food for thought.

When you're suffering you know it's not okay. You know this isn't who or how you're supposed to be. Maybe, you can hardly even look at yourself in the mirror. Let me let you know that I've been there. But you don't have to stay there forever. Yes, acknowledge and accept where you are, you already know that and you need to admit it – it's the first step, admission is Step 1 of the 12 Steps – "We admitted we were powerless over alcohol – that our lives had become unmanageable."

This is how it was first written for Alcoholics Anonymous, but you can try replacing the word "alcohol" with whatever you want. There's more on this to come. But then know that you can move forward to somewhere different, somewhere less dark, somewhere much brighter. Somewhere bright and light and relaxing and full of meaning and happiness. So rest assured, you can do something about it.

I will say to my young children to do their best in life to make it fulfilling, to always be kind, and that maybe those are the same thing. We need to learn to speak to ourselves like this too. Many people are not accustomed to this sort of gentle voice, they grew up with harsh tones. The word gentle here is perfect as it derives from Latin gentilis meaning "of a family or nation, of the same clan".

So much more than beating an addiction, which is clearly a momentous feat in itself, the 12 Steps enable a realisation that allows you to become this person you're supposed to be, by going on a journey to find the hero inside. Consequently significantly emboldened, you can now stand tall, even during the worst periods of life: during a relationship or job rejection; as a loved one suffers with sickness; when the world recoils due to terrorism or a pandemic virus; even during the deaths of your mother and father... You are the one that is there for the others, you are the strong one, you are the brave and courageous, you are the calm in the storm and you are the one from where the light shines in the darkness. Isn't that the aim, to be that one?

It is the enabling of that which can confront the unknown, sometimes the unimaginable, definitely chaos and disorder – and triumph despite it, through it and frequently because of it. It is to be someone who is noble, admirable, excellent and worthy.

From facing what you face, often including your own dark sides, you get something supernatural, something miraculous, something superhuman that you can then pass on to others to change and enhance their lives too. It is wholly transformational. It is being the finder of order within the disorder, finding it and making it grow until it displaces disorder. A hero has to often break the rules of the norm to do this, but they always have to ensure they are a disciplined deviant. You can be that hero time and time again.

We seek some sort of order. Being ready for and overcoming disorder and chaos is the driving force behind many of life's actions. For some people it becomes overwhelming, even the thought of that disorder in life creating debilitating anxiety or panic attacks where we can barely breathe. Depression is when disorder has taken control and is often an attempt to avoid or hide from it.

Many of the problems called mental health issues are attempts at creating order within this disorder, with varying rates of relative sanity to insanity, collapse, fall, ruin and death. Even such as drinking excessively is an attempt at order, that the alcoholic has some control over something. Of course these type of attempts are just deflections and distractions from the reality and will become their own disorder within the main disorder at some point.

There are two words here that can be used to define the difference: "entropy" means "a lack of order, a gradual decline into disorder" (from en- "inside" plus Greek trope meaning "transformation"); and the opposite of entropy is "resolve" meaning "to settle or find a solution to a problem or contentious matter; to decide firmly on a course of action; to have a firm determination to do something".

That is, do you bother to do anything to maintain order, can you make the effort to solve the matters, affairs, concerns and hardships that will happen in life? Psychiatrist M Scott Peck wrote in The Road Less Traveled: "Laziness is love's opposite." Love is an action. This includes self-love. That means, can you find the effort, courage and vitality to deal with life's trials, tests and tribulations as they come at you and as they may well keep coming? Or will you merely keep popping the pills and necking the bottle?

This is why for many people who attend their initial 12 Steps meetings there is a surprise that alcohol or whatever the substance or thing with which they have their addiction problem is rarely (or sometimes not at all) even mentioned. The 12 Steps are about stopping the addiction, but they are at their core about so much more. They are about how to live a full life on life's terms, with a complete sense of meaning and purpose. This is vital or how else can anyone expect not to just get drunk or stoned again or go on a shopping spree that leaves them in debt or gamble money they don't have or work so much they only see their children in the dark when they are sleeping?

The 12 Steps positively answer the fearful doubt that asks: But can I? For those that look in just a little further, that is most often swiftly followed up by the affirmative response to the question: Is there more to life than this then?

In Man's Search For Meaning written by Jewish psychiatrist Viktor Frankl, based on his time in the inhumane Nazi concentration camps, he wrote: "Life ultimately means taking the responsibility to find the right answer to its problems and to fulfil the tasks which it constantly sets for each individual."

The word "responsibility" is key here: it derives from Latin respons meaning "answered, offered in return" from the verb respondere. So we need to know and accept that life will lob and fling things at us, including things that cause suffering. How we respond is how we will be. Our response, what we offer and give, to others and to ourselves, is who we are. That's our courage and our resolve.

What we call a tragedy causes such suffering. The word "tragedy" is from two Greek roots: tragos, meaning "goat" and oide, meaning "ode". So it literally means "goat song", referring to the dramatic plays of the ancient Greeks named such for the actors who dressed in the skins of goats to represent satyrs, goat-like mythological deities, who were lustful, drunken gods. By being lustful and drunk they were causing themselves tragedy and consequently they were suffering, existing constantly under its shadow.

In Shakespeare's tragedy Macbeth, overcome by guilt for her murderous deeds, Lady Macbeth feels agitated, anxious, is unable to eat, rest or sleep – she is irritable, restless and discontent; she is suffering.

Her behaviour disturbs Macbeth, who sends for a doctor to cure his wife. The doctor arrives and quickly recognises the source of Lady Macbeth's problem, so he counters Macbeth's attempt to medicalise his wife's disturbance and says: "This disease is beyond my practice… Infected minds/ To their deaf pillows will discharge their secrets./ More needs she the divine than the physician."

But Macbeth demands the doctor cure his wife: "Canst thou not minister to a mind diseased,/ Pluck from the memory a rooted sorrow,/ Raze out the written troubles of the brain,/ And with some sweet oblivious antidote/ Cleanse the stuffed bosom of that perilous stuff/ Which weighs upon her heart."

But the doctor, knowingly, replies: "Therein the patient/ Must minister to himself."

Frankl wrote that the route to happiness is to find a meaning in life… and that will lead to happiness. The conscious pursuit of happiness undermines happiness. We need meaning.

Addicts obsess, are compulsive and impulsive, all over and over all. Addiction destroys friendships, marriages, partnerships, jobs, careers, childhoods, finances, health, wellbeing, fathers, mothers, sons, daughters, families, communities, cities, nations and life. Although, frequently, an addiction kills someone but refuses to bury them. It's the adversary and opponent within.

Run by ego, that is in a constant state of fear, it is relentless, a continuous cycle of desire and fear. Addiction gives a false meaning. Certainly it is all-consuming: the planning, the getting, the paying, the taking, the recovering, the overall deceitfulness.

In Greek mythology Sisyphus was a king who was punished for his egoistic deceitfulness by being forced to roll a massive boulder up a hill only for it to roll down every time it neared the top, repeating this action for eternity. This is addiction, but it has and will also resonate with people at large for how life sometimes and so frequently seems to be. The 12 Steps create a manner of living, that for addicts and anyone else, allows the rock to be dropped, and the steps taken to reach the top of the hill. And stay there if you wish.

Sometimes the looking up at the top of the hill seems like a journey too far. To even go beyond contemplating it. It just looks like too far to go from where you are, it is too late to set off now is all too often the conclusion. That's why the journey is broken down, a step at a time. (It really is worth the effort because the view at the top is not something to be missed!) It's why the words "one day at a time" and "just for today" are so vital to 12-Step recovery groups, and in fact it's the best way to live life anyway as we are designed this way, to live one day at a time: you could eat so much today that you could eat not even a morsel more, but you will still be hungry tomorrow; similarly, you could sleep for 15 hours tonight, but you'll still want and need to sleep tomorrow night too...

The biblical story of Moses and the half a million or more Israelites who fled across the Red Sea with him from slavery only to find themselves stuck in a wilderness is about this, among some other amazing life lessons. So, trapped in this desolate place they fear they'll starve to death. Moses urges them to have faith, that God will look after them – and sure enough they are provided with a foodstuff that grows on the ground every morning. It gives them all the goodness they need to stay alive. It's termed manna from Heaven.

Moses is instructed by God and passes the message on to the Israelites that all they need to do is gather what they need to eat, one day at a time. Some, as they're fearful they won't be looked after one day at a time, ignore this though and instead gather enough food for the next days. While the others are chatting among themselves and enjoying each other's company in the comfort of the cool shade, they are bending over breaking their backs in the uncomfortable heat. They most likely thought they were being smart, preparing for the worst that was always bound to happen while the others were foolishly just spending pleasant time with their families and friends. But by the next morning all the manna they collected from the day before had turned rotten. And it stank. So then they realised they have to keep faith that they'll always be looked after, one day at a time...

If there are dozens of people telling someone who's suffering under the dark stormy clouds at the base of the hill looking up and thinking they can never reach the sunny uplands, and those people are up at the summit there shouting down at the person who's suffering: "We used to be where you are, exactly there as you are now, in the darkness of the stormy clouds, yet now we are here in the sunlight with this exquisite view and we can help you up... just give us your hand... please..." then why would that person not put out their hand and then hold on tightly for their life?

In The Road Less Traveled, M Scott Peck wrote about this from his experience of trying to help people in his professional and personal life: "The act of love – extending oneself – as I have said, requires a moving out against the inertia of laziness (work) or the resistance engendered by fear (courage). Let us turn now from the work of love to the courage of love. When we extend ourselves, our self enters new and unfamiliar territory, so to speak. Our self becomes a new and different self. We do things we are not accustomed to do. We change. The experience of change, of unaccustomed activity, of being on unfamiliar ground, of doing things differently is frightening. It always was and always will be. People handle their fear of change in different ways, but the fear is inescapable if they are in fact to change."

Stepping up to take the first step and then the next step until you arrive at the top of that hill requires both courage and hard work. It may be that it seems easier to stay at the bottom to neck another bottle or pop another pill. But then you are never going to know that sense of achievement that comes from seeing that far-reaching view, and by reaching the top you will discover who the real you is: perhaps this is the exquisite vision. But until you truly know your valuable worth here on this world, you won't realise how really valuable each one day is, one day at a time; and then until such time you cannot realise how valuable each one day is, and so you will not do anything really valuable with it.

If you expose yourself to something that you are afraid of, that you're avoiding, that you know you need to overcome to reach your aims, if you can face up to those you will undoubtedly be stronger. Then you can keep going up to who knows where –

there are no limits. You can imagine right now that your life would be different and most likely better if you had faced up to those sooner. Let that be a strong incentive right now, and you will get stronger and increasingly stronger, better and increasingly better.

This is for you and for everyone around you too: your friendships, your marriage, your partner, your job and career, finances, for your health, wellbeing, for your father, mother, sons, daughters, childhoods, families, communities, cities, the society that you are a part of, the share of the world that you are in, for nations and life.

Compared to time and in comparison to the universe you, we, are small, we are minuscule, but we are all and everything that we have in this world, on this planet that you have been born into with no say on whether you have that life or not, with no influence on who you are with all your attributes and talents, your shape and size, your features or even what and who you love. Whatever did give us those... you, we, owe it to use what we have been given the best you and we all can.

So while you may be minuscule in the great scheme, on this planet what you do is important, it does matter and it does make a difference – like ripples on a pond radiating outwards. That means you have a responsibility. That's good because it gives life meaning. The alternative is a meaningless lack of conviction, a resigner, destined to be just another one in history who's compliant to the chaos.

Acedia (or "accidie" as an alternative spelling) is an interesting thing. It is from Greek akedia meaning "listlessness", from a- "without" and kedos "care" and it is defined as, variously, a state of lethargy, of not caring about one's position or condition in the world, of spiritual and/or mental sloth, weakness of the will, of being melancholically self-centred; having apathy, boredom, laziness, a feeling of listlessness and dissatisfaction arising from a lack of occupation or excitement, an overwhelming world weariness.

In ancient Greece it meant that a person was in an inert state without pain or care. It's open for a considerably emotional discussion that in the book Your Drug May Be Your Problem by Dr Peter Breggin & Dr David Cohen, which talks about the development of the drugs taken today by people diagnosed with such as depression or anxiety, it says: "…the original 'antipsychotic' drug, Thorazine, was first used by a French surgeon who noticed that it was useful in making surgical patients indifferent or apathetic toward the pain that they were undergoing. There is also evidence that the SSRIs [Selective Serotonin Reuptake Inhibitors] may produce a particular sort of emotional blunting, apathy, and unconcern." When they started using this drug on people with psychosis they upped the doses from what had been given to those recovering from painful surgery. Dr Breggin has described how psychiatric drugs such as these frequently make people taking them "become listless and apathetic". The word "apathy" is derived from Greek apathes meaning "without feeling"; while "listless" is made up of "list" from Old English lystan of Germanic origin from a base meaning "pleasure", and "-less" from Old English leas meaning "devoid of" – so these two words together make for someone who is: without feeling and devoid of pleasure.

Listlessness, in a spiritual sense, was how early Christian monks used the word acedia. The "demon of acedia" had an important rank in early monastic demonology – the study of evil spirit – and early psychology. For example, Evagrius the Solitary, a Christian monk, stated in the 4th Century that it was "the most troublesome" of the eight kinds of evil thoughts listed at the time in his community. Acedia was seen as a temptation, and the great peril was in not resisting it and so falling into its deep trap. It became known as "the midday demon" for obvious reasons.

Also in the 4th Century, it was described by another Christian monk, John the Ascetic, how it could "take possession of some unhappy soul" and how a person consumed with it would be someone who "frequently gazes up at the sun, as if it was too slow in setting, and so a kind of unreasonable confusion of mind takes possession of him like some foul darkness" until that person is "worn out by the spirit of acedia, as by some strong battering ram...".

It became a word meaning "a restless way of being and with an inability to work or pray". Theologian Thomas Aquinas described acedia in the 13th Century as "the sorrow of the world", that it was the opposite of "spiritual joy" and "one opposite is known through the other, as darkness through light. Hence also what evil is must be known from the nature of good."

It is in Dante's 14th Century epic poem Divine Comedy not only as a sin of the damned but also as the sin that leads Dante to the edge of Hell itself. In Dante's vision, those who have sinned with acedia seem to have landed themselves in the Mount of Purgatory terrace with the Wrathful. Trapped in a saturnine bog their cries come bubbling up to the surface: "'We were sullen in the sweet air that is gladdened by the sun, bearing in our hearts a sluggish smoke; now we are sullen in the black mire.' This hymn they gurgle in their throat, for they cannot get the words out plainly."

As well in that century, Chaucer's parson in The Canterbury Tales includes acedia in his list of vices: "For Envye blindeth the herte of a man, and Ire troubleth a man; and Accidie maketh him hevy, thoghtful, and wrawe./ Envye and Ire maken bitternesse in herte; which bitternesse is moder of Accidie, and binimeth him the love of alle goodnesse."

It is interesting that Chaucer's parson links anger and envy with the acedia that will diminish the love of all goodness. Of the seven deadly sins it seems it is most generally regarded as being within the bounds of sloth, but it is known as in fact being something more than laziness. How well does that tie in with M Scott Peck writing that: "Laziness is love's opposite."

Acedia can be viewed as being in the aura that's the absolute opposite of having joie de vivre. Having acedia means that someone crushed underneath it does not even care that they do not care. It is negativity, cynicism, pessimism, rejection, denial, disbelief, hopelessness, scepticism, agnosticism, lack of conviction and absence of moral values. This is an overall dominating despair that frequently ends in suicide – although even that can be too much to bother with, because acedia is such a tragic pitiful state it believes in not a single thing, cares not about anything or anybody, neither loves or hates nothing, has lost purpose for everything, and only stays alive because there's damn all over which it's worth the effort of dying. It's a darker shade of black, the goth blues, it's something hotter than an uncontrollable fire, darker that a desert new-moon night, more acrid than thick smoke, more alone than a faraway star, it's like trying to breathe with a lung only the size of a teabag. It's a fate that's probably far worse than death.

In more recent times it has been used in connection with depression. In the past century author Ian

Fleming, writer of those classic Hero's Journey stories James Bond, wrote about acedia. It's been reported that Fleming advised his children: "Never say 'no' to adventures. Always say 'yes', otherwise you'll lead a very dull life." But he knew his own heartaches, and it was said by his mistress that the author was "a man in a serious depression". Others who knew the Flemings said there was depression about in the family. Ian Fleming died from a heart attack aged 56 on his son Caspar's 12th birthday. Then, after four spells in the psychiatric unit of a hospital where he was treated for depression, Caspar died aged only 23. The verdict recorded his death as suicide while suffering from depression. A psychiatrist told the inquest: "He was a rather moody and pessimistic man… and he felt strongly that he had not got a proper place in life."

In addition, in the early 20th Century, author and philosopher Aldous Huxley wrote about acedia, in which he makes a point that can be seen to say that as humankind has given way to an increased search for meaning and purpose in materialism, so too has there been an increase in acedia: a world weariness, of which such as depression, anxiety and addiction are symptoms. "For clearly the progress of accidie is a spiritual event of considerable importance. How is it to be explained? It is not as though the nineteenth century invented accidie. Boredom, hopelessness and despair have always existed, and have been felt as poignantly in the past as we feel them now. … The mal du siècle was an inevitable evil; indeed, we can claim with a certain pride that we have a right to our accidie. With us it is not a sin or a disease of the hypochondrias; it is a state of mind which fate has forced upon us."

More recently, the Manic Street Preachers sang about the invasion of being that is acedia in their song Of Walking Abortion on 1994's album The Holy Bible.
"Life is lead weights, pendulum died,
Pure or lost, spectator or crucified,
Recognised truth acedia's blackest hole,
Junkies, winos, whores; the nation's moral suicide."

It was written while lyricist and rhythm guitarist Richey Edwards was self-harming and struggling with depression, alcohol abuse and anorexia nervosa. By the time of the album's release, he was hospitalised in a London mental health hospital. On 1 February 1995, he disappeared after parking his car close to the Severn Bridge. It is assumed he ended his life.

As with many people who are in the grips of addiction, the co-founders of Alcoholics Anonymous, Bill W and Dr Bob, could have easily fallen prey to the state of acedia. Maybe they were for periods of their disease, but if they were – thank God for this world that they found a way out of it. Although there has been the birth of dozens of 12-Step groups such as Al-Anon (offering a programme of recovery for the families and friends of alcoholics, formed in 1951), Narcotics Anonymous (1953),

Gamblers Anonymous (1957), Overeaters Anonymous (1960), Debtors Anonymous (1971), Emotions Anonymous (1971), Sex and Love Addicts Anonymous (1976), Cocaine Anonymous (1982), Workaholics Anonymous (1983), Co-Dependents Anonymous/CoDA (1986), and Internet and Technology Addicts Anonymous (2009), it is AA that remains the largest 12-Step group with two million members in 180 countries.

Its beginnings are one of extraordinary synchronicity, as if it had to happen... It is in itself a remarkable Hero's Journey story...

Bill W started life in Vermont in the USA, where he was abandoned by both his parents. By his teens he was a rebellious young man who suffered from bouts of depression. His depression worsened, soon coupled with panic attacks. By his early 20s he had discovered alcohol and was soon drinking to pass out. After military service, he failed to graduate from law school because he was too drunk to pick up his diploma. His drinking likewise adversely affected his working life in his chosen career as a stockbroker. In the next few years he ended up in hospital due to his heavy drinking. He was told by doctors that he would either die from his drinking or have to be locked up permanently due to getting a "wet brain" that would likely cause him extreme confusion, dementia and loss of muscle coordination.

Meanwhile, in 1931 a business executive called Rowland Hazard had sought treatment for alcoholism with leading psychiatrist Carl Jung in Switzerland. When Hazard ended treatment with Jung after a year, he resumed drinking and consequently returned for more treatment. But Jung told Hazard that his case, as with other alcoholics, was nearly hopeless – and that his only hope might be a life-changing "vital spiritual experience" – something that Jung regarded as a phenomenon. Jung also advised Hazard that his connection with a church did not mean the necessary vital spiritual experience that he needed.

So Hazard returned to America where he went to an Oxford Group meeting. The Oxford Group was founded by American Christian missionary Frank Buchman who believed that the root of all human personal problems was fear and selfishness. With the group's help, Hazard managed to stay sober by gaining the spiritual conversion that Jung had suggested as the only chance for people drinking like him.

The Oxford Group's experience was that a new convert needed to win over other converts to preserve their own conversion. With that in mind, Hazard brought a man called Ebby Thacher to the group. In keeping with the conversion suggestion of trying to pass it on, Thacher in turn contacted his old schoolfriend Bill W, who he knew still had a drinking problem.

With his career now in ruins due to his excessive drinking, Bill W was a forlorn figure when Thacher visited him at his apartment. When Thacher said "he had got religion" it has been described how Bill W's heart sank because he had struggled believing in God. Yet of that meeting with Thacher, Bill W later wrote: "My friend suggested what then seemed a novel idea. He said, 'Why don't you choose your own conception of God?' That statement hit me hard. It melted the icy intellectual mountain in whose shadow I had lived and shivered many years."

When Thacher left that day though, Bill W continued to drink excessively. Back in hospital once more, he was given a drug concoction known as the Belladonna Cure that caused hallucinations. While in bed there, in utter despair, he cried out: "I'll do anything! Anything at all! If there be a God, let Him show Himself!"

He had then the sensation of a bright light and what he said was "an ecstasy beyond description".

Thacher visited Bill W at the hospital again and introduced him to the basic tenets of the Oxford Group as well as to The Varieties Of Religious Experience by psychologist William James. Bill W read that James thought spiritual conversions came from calamities, and that their source lies in pain and hopelessness.

This was not a new human thought: written at the Gates of Hell in Dante's Divine Comedy are the words: "Abandon all hope, you who enter here." It's from the first part of the poem, called Inferno (Italian for Hell), where Hell is depicted as nine concentric circles of torment located within the Earth: it is the "realm ... of those who have rejected spiritual values..." Dante's guide through Hell, the Roman poet Virgil, tells him the inhabitants of this infernal region are "those who have lost the good of intellect; the substance of evil, the loss of humanity, intelligence, goodwill, and the capacity to love". Perhaps, then, they knew more about these matters several centuries ago...

Indeed, Carl Jung's psychology contained a great amount based on the fact that the prime symbolic composition of religious convictions were the stories that if understood and taken heed of would allow us to progress through our lives as self-assured people, responsible and courageous, even when confronted with disorder, as we will be in life because it is as much a part of life as order.

Sensing some order in his life, Bill W started then going to Oxford Group meetings and socialising with other ex-drinking Oxford Group people. He became especially taken by their spiritual ideals of the "Four Absolutes": Absolute Honesty, Absolute Purity, Absolute Unselfishness, Absolute Love. Even so, after a while he stopped going to the Oxford Group meetings and started on a task to save other alcoholics, visiting such as local hospitals to find people he could help.

But of all the alcoholics Bill W initially tried to help, not one stayed sober. Then on a business trip in Ohio, he was tempted to throw away his sobriety himself. He stood there in a hotel foyer, craving a drink. With increasing anxiety he contemplated his choices: talk to another alcoholic in an attempt to stay sober or get it over with by getting a drink in the hotel bar... Order or chaos?

He found himself standing by a phone booth there, and he started a series of phone calls that put him in touch with a surgeon called Dr Bob. This doctor agreed to meet him, inviting him to his home, but he'd only give him 15 minutes, not a second more. This despite the fact that Dr Bob's medical practice and family life were in grave jeopardy. For 17 years his daily routine had been to force himself not to drink until the afternoon, and then to get drunk, crash out until he woke up and took sedatives to calm his morning jitters.

However Bill W's understanding of alcoholism and his ability to share from his own experience meant that 15 minutes stretched to six hours. Soon, Bill W moved into Dr Bob's home and from there, both men made plans to take their message of recovery on the road.

After three years of trial and error, and after a large amount of failure in getting alcoholics to recover, three successful groups had emerged in America – the first in Akron, the second in New York and the third in Cleveland. By this time in 1939, the recoveries from alcoholism numbered about 100, and the burgeoning association set down its guidelines and experiences in the book called Alcoholics Anonymous that was mostly written by Bill W. Nicknamed the "Big Book" due to the thickness of the paper initially used, the groups got their name: Alcoholics Anonymous. In it, for the first time, the spiritual solution was written as the 12 Steps and made available to all.

So the 12 Steps were born – and a phenomenal Hero's Journey had also just taken place. That journey continues when you consider that it took almost two years to sell the initial 4,650 copies of the book's first printing. Yet it has now sold more than 30 million copies and been translated into 67 languages.

The 12 Steps are about how to have a spiritual awakening and Alcoholics Anonymous says of the spiritual condition: "… we have been not only mentally and physically ill, we have been spiritually sick. When the spiritual malady is overcome, we straighten out mentally and physically." When people look inside, this spiritual element of their disease becomes clear.

"It has to hurt if it's to heal."

"It was really scary… but then it was beautiful."

The Neverending Story sentence and my son Daniel's statement both also summarise the Hero's

Journey, the universal story structure that's shared by stories worldwide, a common blueprint of a broad category of tales that always reveal a conversion, a life-changing transformation. The term Hero's Journey was coined in 1949 by a professor of literature called Joseph Campbell. Sometimes also known as the "monomyth", Campbell was referring to a wide-ranging type of story in which a character ventures out to get what they need, faces conflict – and ultimately triumphs over adversity.

And in doing so they discover something magical, something extraordinary, that was always inside them that they never would have discovered without their calamity, without the adversity, without embarking on the adventure. Campbell studied story structures and he spotted that there were similar theme structures and symbolism in stories from cultures and civilisations separated by space and time throughout the history of humankind – from the Greek myths and biblical stories to legends, bestsellers and Hollywood blockbusters. The Neverending Story is one such exceptional story, the film based on the novel of the same name by Michael Ende. As well, the Hero's Journey is in some board games and more recently in many video and computer games.

Influenced by Jung's view of myths, Campbell described in his 1949 book The Hero With A Thousand Faces that the basic narrative Hero's Journey pattern was: "A hero ventures forth from the world of common day into a region of supernatural wonder: fabulous forces are there encountered and a decisive victory is won: the hero comes back from this mysterious adventure with the power to bestow boons on his fellow man."

But they can only gain said boons by going to where they least want to go: by entering the innermost part of the darkest cave guarded by the most fearsome dragon they can imagine – and even not quite imagine such is the terror it holds. But then they must slay that dragon. They can then claim the treasure there.

This is the truth for all of us… Where you least want to go is where you will find that which you most need.

It is when you confront the unknown. An inner journey into the unconscious mind, to the centre of the Earth, to the core of the Universe, into the heart and soul of the Spirit. It is the struggle of consciousness up to the light. That which you fear and avoid, that which you abhor, that which revolts you, which makes you feel nausea, that thing in the darkest shadows, those things, your shadow side, that which you fight from going anywhere near at all costs, that is where you need to go to get that for which you are crying out.

Hero's Journey stories are about letting you know where you should go and how you need to be in this world. Jung thought many of the common themes in stories are in a part of everyone as what he termed the "collective unconscious". His belief was that the mind was made up of three parts: the ego represents the conscious mind as it is made up of the memories, thoughts and emotions of which someone has awareness; then the personal unconscious is all the information that's present in someone's mind, but that is memories that have been repressed or forgotten.

It's the remaining part that's the most important to stories – that is, the idea that a section of the deepest unconscious mind is inherited and not shaped by personal experience. Jung believed that the collective unconscious was a collection of knowledge and images passed on from our earliest human ancestors and that every person has within them at birth.

It is why on hearing, reading and watching these stories there is a strange sense of déjà vu, a feeling of knowing this is the Truth. Deep inside, floating there powerfully, there is the perception: "I know this from somewhere..." This could be because human beings are self-conscious and so we have been watching ourselves for tens of thousands of years. We have been trying to figure out ourselves and this world we live in.

We are different, but we don't vitally change in any way. Someone from thousands of years ago, in a world and society completely different to ours, still felt the pangs of romantic heartbreak and the anger of injustice and the joy of listening to music and the love of seeing children play, they still felt all of those exactly as we do.

Ancient books and more recent old books tell us this. You only need to look at some of the titles of the Anglo-Saxon poems from 960 to 990 that are collected in the Exeter Book: The Wanderer, Vainglory, The Ruin, The Wife's Lament, and The Fates Of Mortals. Reading them confirms it – for instance, in The Wanderer it writes of a modcearig man, meaning a man "troubled in mind" who meditates on past hardships and on the fact that mass killings have been innumerable in history, and finally as the snottor on mode (man wise in mind) who has come to understand that life is transient and full of adversities and suffering, and that strength and security only lives with God. This Old English word modcearig if looked into is revealing as mod was used to mean "mind, spirit, courage, soul, heart, mood" (it's from here that this latter word developed); then cearig was used to mean "sad, sorrowful, dire, anxious, cautious". We don't vitally change in any way.

It is for this reason, that we are all innately and intricately the same, that anyone (with the human condition) who does the 12 Steps thoroughly, honestly and fearlessly will get the result stated emphatically in Step 12: a "spiritual awakening".

The collective unconscious involves cognitive structures that Jung termed "archetypes", which cannot be observed directly but that instead manifest as various images or patterns that form the basis of many myths and stories. They are also familiar in other creative forms such as poetry, lyrics, photography and art. (Thank God for these creations and their creators as they help us perhaps much more than is realised in this modern world: such as that even the name of the musical genre "the blues" indicates, it coming it is believed from the expression "blue devils" used to describe the intense hallucinations of alcohol withdrawal, and before then blue devils was the name for the demons that many thought caused depression.) Jung suggested that these archetypes are reflections of aspects of the human mind. He noticed a striking similarity between the dreams of his patients and the common archetypes of mythology, and he suggested that both were coming from a deeper source, in the "collective unconscious" of humankind.

Archetypes are components of our collective unconscious and serve to organise, direct and inform human thought and behaviour. They are instincts of the mind and soul that can be portrayed as a character type, a theme, a symbol or even a setting. "Most fundamentally, an archetype is a behavioural pattern and the reflection of that behaviour in a story," is how psychologist Jordan Peterson puts it.

Soldier, author and anthropologist Lord Raglan devised the "mythic hero archetype" in his 1936 book The Hero, A Study In Tradition, Myth And

Drama. He stated that heroes and their stories around the world and throughout history have 22 traits that include: unusual conception circumstances; brought up by foster parents in a distant country; defeats a king/giant/dragon/beast; and meets a mysterious death. Using "Lord Raglan's scale" it is that such as Oedipus gets 21 out of 22; Krishna, 21; King Arthur, 19; and Robin Hood, 13.

More recently, psychologists have identified the characteristics of heroes – Elaine Kinsella and colleagues established in 2015 that a hero most usually has bravery, moral integrity, courage, conviction, honesty, is altruistic, self-sacrificing, selfless, determined, protecting, inspiring, helpful, humble and proactive. Scott T Allison and George R Goethals, psychologists and authors of Heroes: What They Do And Why We Need Them, state that heroes are wise, strong, resilient, reliable, charismatic, caring, selfless and inspiring. Heroes appeal to us as they give us wisdom; enhance us; provide moral modelling; and they offer protection (the word "hero" is from Greek heros meaning "protector").

This explains similarities in stories from cultures that were separated. These are stories of humans and human evolvement that are deeply embedded. For instance, everywhere from Africa and the Americas to Asia, Europe and Oceania has had a great flood story, whereby a flood is sent by a deity or deities to destroy a civilisation as an act of divine retribution for breaking the moral codes.

This flood myth motif is found among so many cultures throughout history, including among the Mesopotamians (with the Epic Of Gilgamesh, an epic poem from 4,000 years ago, one of the oldest written stories we know about – and that is considered one of the first Hero's Journey stories put in writing as well as the second oldest known religious text, after the Egyptian Pyramid Texts). As well it's found in the stories of the ancient Greeks, Hinduism, Chinese mythology, Norse mythology, the Maya peoples and Australian Aborigines.

The one most of us know today of course is the Bible's Genesis flood story about Noah and his ark. This story shows God wanted to return the Earth to its pre-Creation state of watery chaos by flooding it because of humanity's corrupt way of living – and then remake it using the microcosm of Noah's ark. The narrative explains the evil of mankind that moved God to destroy the world by the way of the flood. It's the battle between good and evil, a world of order and chaos.

The flooding is often accompanied by strong tumultuous storms that can represent such as rage, grief, pain, anxiety, fear... Frequently when we're in these feelings we feel as if we cannot breathe, that we are choking, akin to being up to our necks in it, or our noses just about poking out as we are starting to drown in the chaotic water that surrounds us. Water also signifies birth, as babies are when in the womb's amniotic fluid; and it also represents cleansing, washing away all the dirt and impurities to reveal the pure new.

Interestingly the name Noah means "rest, repose" and he was a person who tried to live a righteous life by God's will rather than by his own will. So he was a person who God knew would respond well.

There is a connection to the name Noah then – "repose" meaning "a state of tranquility" – and the coming out the other side from the flood with the words from pages 83-84 of Alcoholics Anonymous known as the "9th step promises": "We are going to know a new freedom and a new happiness. We will not regret the past nor wish to shut the door on it. We will comprehend the word serenity and we will know peace. No matter how far down the scale we have gone, we will see how our experience can benefit others. That feeling of uselessness and self-pity will disappear. We will lose interest in selfish things and gain interest in our fellows. Self-seeking will slip away. Our whole attitude and outlook upon life will change. Fear of people and of economic insecurity will leave us. We will intuitively know how to handle situations which used to baffle us. We will suddenly realise that God is doing for us what we could not do for ourselves. Are these extravagant promises? We think not. They are being fulfilled among us – sometimes quickly, sometimes slowly. They will always materialise if we work for them."

These stories and myths then help us when we fall into the unknown, that has so often been represented as floods or as the underworld in mythology. They show us that if we can find the divine spark within we can play our part, a big part, in ensuring we don't return to the watery chaos. If we live by the Best Ideal, the Highest Good or God, then we avoid the corruption – the breaking of the moral code – that always leads back to chaos. Without fail, that's where it goes. It can't go any other place as it goes against how we are designed for living. So far, humanity has never been able to stay on the straight path for long… The myths and Hero's Journey stories and 12 Steps show us how we can, why we need to and what we can do if we realise we are starting to walk the wrong way.

Humankind's battle is always against chaos. Avoiding chaos; getting out of chaos; seeking order from chaos. Failure of love is a sad and terrible chaos. You are a small child and you look up at those huge God-like faces upon whom you are entirely dependent, because young humans are born far earlier in developmental terms than most animals – but instead of love you are terrified to realise that their ears are plugged up to hear nothing; the eyes are glaring with disdain; and rather than being loving, the noises that come from their mouths are loud and abrupt, jagged harsh biting barks that come from impatience, intolerance, laziness and all other forms of selfishness: no-love. In the worst cases, the love that is needed is instead violent acts of despicable malevolence.

The word "order" derives from Latin ordiri meaning "begin". But as there is no concept of light without also having dark, there is no order without chaos. Corruption – meaning "to change from good to bad in morals, manners, or actions; a departure from the original or from what is pure" is from Latin com rumpere meaning "to break" – it is the fall from order into chaos. The myths and Hero's Journey stories, as do the 12 Steps, reveal to us a way to avoid falling into or falling back into chaos, into that unfathomable bottomless gulf – but also how to restore order from chaos if we fall again.

Author, journalist and philanthropist Mitch Albom wrote in Tuesdays With Morrie: "Life is a series of pulls back and forth... A tension of opposites, like a pull on a rubber band. Most of us live somewhere in the middle. A wrestling match... Which side wins? Love wins. Love always wins."

Some say we need to learn in life how to walk the fine line between order and chaos: not so far in to order that we die of boredom, become too controlling and never have anything to grow from; yet not to fall too far for too long into chaos, which is where we can sometimes find that which we need to renew or develop, or we may get stuck there and end up dead.

No life will be without some chaos, that is simply never going to happen, for everybody gets something. Life could be considered in terms of a graph as a stretched-out spring that goes, ideally, from bottom left (Birth) to top right (Death) with the x-axis showing Age and the y-axis for Spiritual & Emotional Growth. The top of each spring loop is order, the bottom is chaos. The rising curves up to the top of each loop of the uncoiled spring indicate the growth that we make that returns us to order, and the lower parts are showing Life during a drop into chaos. So there is throughout Life going to be a repeated loop of order into chaos. But if growth happens in the chaos, from what we learn in that chaos, the rise is made to the top of the uncoiled spring's next loop. As Age goes up so then does Spiritual & Emotional Growth. However, for many people's graph, the uncoiled spring will maybe stop its general rise at a certain age, which is frequently some time before adulthood. For some, the uncoiled spring drops right down to the graph's baseline and there is so little growth that it gets so stretched downwards it becomes a virtually straight wire. They are stuck at a much lower spiritual and emotional place than they should be for their age. If this uncoiled spring gets pulled too harshly, without any growth, it can fall below the baseline, a shaded area marked Death.

Abuse, trauma, toxic shame – these failures of love – all abruptly and brutally shove people a long way down into chaos. If this happens in what's supposed to be sweet innocent childhood, then when we become old enough, usually as teens, we often have to escape, and then we likely meet a new chaos. It's supremely difficult to find order if you have never known what order is. Even when someone who's been brutally forced into chaos can create what seems like order on the outside, the chaos continues to swirl like a self-destructive whirlwind on the inside, until they go inwards to deal with this. When there is internal chaos like this there is often an external attempt to create order. This is often desperate and frantic and it is behind much addiction and other mental health conditions, as well as many political conflicts and wars.

Anxiety and panic attacks frequently grab hold at the mere thought of potential chaos in the outside world; if we drink excessively it's because of chaos or to temporarily deceive ourselves that it isn't there: the apparent choice of any addiction is a deception of having some order. "Deceive" derives from Latin decipere meaning "catch, ensnare, cheat". The battle in addictions is the war to avoid or fight the chaos, to remain in or regain order. It is always a deception.

It can be seen as an unbroken fall from order through corruption into chaos. There was the Beginning, then there was the Fall... It's hugely symbolic of the human condition. So far, overall, it is the human condition.

After the Beginning, the rest of the Bible, as in the rest of life, is about the need to be in order. As with many religious books, as with myths and all Hero's Journey stories, as with the 12 Steps, these are guides written by other human beings – with divine inspiration and through absolute love – that seek to show us how we can achieve that order and maintain it. They are guidebooks on how to live life on life's terms using all that has been designed within and about us.

A relationship break-up is chaos (especially if you're cheated on), so is the loss of a job, a virus pandemic, racism, bullying, a serious sickness, bereavement and war. If there is already chaos inside, these can shake it up so much that everything feels now so utterly out of control that a breakdown of sorts is highly possible. Drink, prescribed or illegal drugs, work, sex, gambling, overeating and other addictions can never really work, not in any enduring or real manner, because what they are attempting to do is create order in place of the chaos. But they are two separate things, order and chaos – they are opposites. So getting stoned, getting drunk, working excessively and so on is the equivalent of putting chaos in a net. Yes, it may be in a net, contained – but as it's chaos it always has a chance to break free. It is still chaos and the net cannot hold it forever because chaos is unpredictable and unknown: its very nature is disorder, disarray, confusion, mayhem, pandemonium… If anyone thinks they can control all of that, with anything like this, good luck but no. Chaos will always break out at some point. If you are trying to control it through such as drink and drugs and so on, I have the feeling it can break out at will. As it says in AA's Big Book about alcohol, it is "cunning, baffling and powerful".

Order is not chaos, and putting chaos in a net does not and never will transform chaos into order.

Those who survive these sort of life events and then thrive the most are those who can swiftly confront the dragon of chaos to create a brand-new order. So in such as the case of discovering a partner has cheated on you, you could work on your physical and emotional wellbeing, learn some new skills, step up in any roles you have in life such as being a mother or a work team leader, do other estimable things that boost your self-esteem: become someone who is ready for love again who believes they deserve love. Or you could stay in the chaos and get drunk a lot in a bid to block it all out, in the faint hope that the dragon will go away. It won't and it will slay you unless you slay it first.

On relationships, only a narcissist or some badly damaged person in another way wants a "romantic" relationship where their partner agrees with their every word and action, and so where they never learn from each other, they never grow. Perhaps, with this in mind, our romantic relationships are merely a microcosmic imitation of how our relationship with a greater power is or ought to be. It's been said that an alcoholic is looking at the bottom of every glass they ever drink to see if love is there. Carl Jung in a letter to AA co-founder Bill W described alcoholism, paraphrased, as "a low-level thirst for God", and then maybe there is understanding of the signs commonly seen around churches that say: "God is love". Just try putting the word "love" for "God", and this has worked for many people who have problems with saying God. Love is God.

Heroes are those who get the real information and develop the belief they can defeat the dragon of chaos, and then find the honour and courage to do it, as represented in myths and stories for centuries, such as with Saint George slaying the dragon – which is why nations including England, Ethiopia and Georgia claim him as representative of their national identity. People like people with knowledge, belief, honour and courage. We can all be this person, for that capability is in us all. We all have that power.

Again, perhaps our ancestors knew a damned sight more about all of this centuries ago than many of us do now dressed up in the intellectual armour of this modern scientific age of profits over prophets. That intellectual armour, slammed tightly on to someone by prideful ego, often has a visor that's fixed so stubbornly it cannot be budged a fraction to even glance at anything that could possibly be to do with spirit. This ego's armour is all too often doggedly worn right into an early grave.

How long then can anyone possibly cheat chaos? Well, numbness means no feeling or sense of either order or chaos, but it also means no life, at least certainly not the life that was intended. Being always busy (and "important" and "essential") is another form of numbness from it. But it's a bloody rough battle every second to keep that up. Ask the business executive, in recovery from a heart attack or other stress-related disease, with tubes and wires keeping them alive. Addicts in recovery realise this and will tell you that their worst day in recovery is better than any day in addiction.

Fear creates chaos; love is order. Then what is love? Corinthians in the Bible has this: "Love is patient, love is kind. It does not envy, it does not boast, it is not proud. It does not dishonour others, it is not self-seeking, it is not easily angered, it keeps no record of wrongs. Love does not delight in evil but rejoices with the truth. It always protects, always trusts, always hopes, always perseveres. Love never fails." Sometimes love has to fight, like a hot fever to banish the virus. The original angels were not the cherubby rosy-cheeked plump babies with wings as they are most often portrayed nowadays: they were more like a formidable spiritual security force, and if they had to fight they did fight. And the evil they fought would know about it.

Jordan Peterson makes the point that "the antidote to chaos is the balance between chaos and order" and he wrote in 12 Rules For Life: An Antidote to Chaos "...the great myths and religious stories of the past, particularly those derived from an earlier, oral tradition, were moral in their intent, rather than descriptive. Thus, they did not concern themselves with what the world was, as a scientist might have it, but with how a human being should act. I suggested

that our ancestors portrayed the world as a stage –
a drama – instead of a place of objects. I described
how I had come to believe that the constituent
elements of the world as drama were order and
chaos, and not material things."

There is order and there are, as I see it, three
different types of chaos, all aspects of the same but
varying degrees of disorder, and they all need to be
dealt with in the same way – by confronting as
swiftly as is possible if we are to grow and move
forwards in life to make and maintain our greatest
ideal.

So do we always need to walk the fine line between
order and chaos? Or is it that we try to stay in order,
but sometimes choose to try something and then
some chaos can arise from that? This is then
"ordered chaos", as there was a decision made
within order, and some sort of chaos would likely
have been considered or even expected, such as
when leaving home, starting a family, a new
business, travelling, going to help somewhere that's
suffered an earthquake or war... It is chaos that
might well arise as an attempt to create some new
sort of order.

We can undoubtedly learn from things that happen
in this world, and often when it is painful, then that
suffering gets us to focus more intently and more
swiftly. This way, we learn and make changes and
grow as quickly as possible. That must be needed
then. But does a loving God, sometimes called the

Father, really want us to be continually walking that fine line between order and chaos? That would seem, surely, to be a way of living that would be exhausting, that would require lots of our energy, more like using constant willpower, a misuse of it – and that would take much of our potency that could be used for other things, especially loving and caring for others. The Greatest Commandment says: "'Love the Lord your God with all your heart and with all your soul and with all your mind and with all your strength.' The second is this: 'Love your neighbour as yourself.' There is no commandment greater than these."

If I, as with all human beings, am created in the image and likeness of God, and I look at how I want life to be for my children... Then no, I really don't want them that much on the edge all the time: that would seem to be perpetual stress. It would take too much of their heart and soul and mind and it would take it too often. So I would like for them to live most of the time in an ordered world, somewhere they feel secure and not always anxious about when the next fall might happen. I would like for them to realise and have the ability to make their choices, so long as they are living morally, many of them if that's what they wish, without any fear but in the knowledge that these choices might sometimes lead to some "ordered chaos".

For, of course, a life lived totally in order where we could predict the future would not be fulfilling, and it would get downright boring. That is being stuck in a job you hate for years of your life, for example. Who the hell would want that life for their children? Or want for them to be living under a totalitarian regime. I am certain that God doesn't want it for any of us, God's children, either. The Exodus story in the Bible is saying, among many considerable things, that God doesn't want us to be slaves. Remember, it is not God that has made these systems where such as tedious work exists in a system that throws a hangman's noose of debt round people's necks; it is not God making dictators. What makes these things – some call it the Satanic system – is free will, and giving it our permission.

God knows, I really want my boys to fearlessly try such as new ventures at something they love and that would best use their talents, to travel the world, maybe even the universe is possible when they are older, and to have their own children. But then that they can be well informed and have enough integrity and courage to deal with any ordered chaos if and when it arises.

Likewise, when in life the dragon of chaos looms suddenly, that is nothing to do with their choices – then that they can step forward with no fear to confront it and move on, and in doing so grow, and that they will share their wisdom and courage and the knowledge of being fearless. Absolute love. I think this is what a Higher Power, God, wants for us all. To be fearless with this gift of life. To be our best ideal. To have the most energy and potency we can to love one another and to love ourselves enough to care for ourselves. It is only fear that stops us being this way. God is love, fear is the adversary.

As well as ordered chaos (expected chaos) and, let's call it, "disordered chaos" (unexpected chaos) that comes at us from external events such as a partner leaving us, a job loss or bereavement, there is chaos that is a certainty when anyone lives outside the moral code that we all know from inside ourselves, as we're made this way – although some people have definitely deeply buried it. We're made this way because otherwise human beings would have imploded a long, long time ago. So such as living with excessive pride, self-pity, self-centredness, selfish lust, selfishness, intolerance, impatience, jealousy, greed and gluttony – these will always lead to "corrupt chaos". Corrupt chaos will always create something very bad. Perhaps not immediately, but it will come. It is like a progressive disease. If not stopped it is often fatal, with a great amount of pain.

When too many individuals in a society or a nation live in a way that breaks the moral code like this there is always corrupt chaos. On a national level it frequently ends in war. The history of humankind so far has been Order, Corruption, Chaos. Too many individuals cannot resist the temptations and fail the tests and trials. The Creative Intelligence surely doesn't want it like this. (Unless we are the playthings of the Gods, looking down on us for entertainment as they watch this world as a soap opera with characters run by various dominant dysfunctional emotions. What a show we give them!)

It's a spiritual law equivalent of jumping from a high pier into the sea, that causes as you go under the water an ordered chaos until you resurface; but if instead you are pushed in by someone that is disordered chaos; and if you jump in with a heavy boulder strapped to you, that's the equivalent of corrupt chaos. (In case you're wondering, if someone pushes you in after having strapped a boulder to you, that's disordered corrupt chaos…) There are physical laws in life, and spiritual laws operate in a similar manner. If you live in one way or another, they are inescapable.

To restore order, whatever form, we must then confront chaos, however it arises – but always as soon as it arises unless we want to be thrown around by it. One way is to remember that in many myths and stories, the order was created from chaos through the power of good words. As well as what you say, these can be those words going on inside your head. As it says in the Bible: "For as he thinketh in his heart, so is he…" Or in the Bhagavad Gita: "You are what you believe in. You become that which you believe you can become." Or Shakespeare's words in Hamlet: "There is nothing either good or bad, but thinking makes it so."

We always have a choice with our thoughts: they can be our friend, or they can be our enemy. How revealing it is to realise the word Satan is from

Hebrew meaning "adversary" and "plot against". That's exactly what our thoughts are and do to us if we let them – all this going on in your head: "You'd never be good enough", "Not you!", "You don't have enough experience", "You're too old", "You're too fat", "You're too skinny", "You look so ugly", "You're not smart enough", "They're so much better than me", "Who could ever love a person like me?","Who do you think you are!", "No way that you could do that" and so on. If a friend repeatedly said this sort of criticism to you, you'd certainly decide to unfriend them! As a child, appallingly and shockingly, many parents are exactly like this, projecting their toxic thoughts and feelings on and into their offspring, most likely following the family blueprint that might be traced back to when their ancestors lived in caves. No wonder that family group has always struggled and suffered in some way. No wonder that child as an adult walks around continually battering themselves around the head from what is continually hammering away at them inside their head.

It is one of the reasons the group therapy of the 12-Step meetings and that is encouraged at many rehab centres is so effective: it recreates the loving family that was missing. It is the first time many of the people have been in a group where their emotions are listened to and cared about, it's the first time they have known choices to be discussed and their opinion valued, it is the first time for many that they may have been shown love.

Many, for instance, at the more expensive rehab centres might have financial wealth beyond most people's wildest dreams and in their working environment have many people answering to them, but not necessarily really wanting to listen to them. These are very wealthy people who are deeply troubled, and this, as is so often the case, can be traced back to childhood. For instance, many were packed off as children to live at a boarding school, because that is in the family blueprint (along with possibly aloof, superior or arrogant ways of thinking and behaving). I cannot imagine how anyone thinks sending a child away from their family home like this gives a good, positive and loving message to that child. The completing of this insanity is that the parents sending their children off most likely know all of this because they were sent away exactly like that too.

Nobody wants this harshness. What we all really want is gentle love.

Mitch Albom got this in Tuesdays With Morrie: "The truth is, when our mothers held us, rocked us, stroked our heads – none of us ever got enough of that. We all yearn in some way to return to those days when we were completely taken care of – unconditional love, unconditional attention. Most of us didn't get enough."

Some not only didn't get enough: they didn't get any, and then they got the opposite of that too. Children who come from a broken home that took several years breaking up before their eyes and in their ears will often have seen little in the way of love, empathy and kindness; poverty may have been an issue as their parents feuded, and with it a lack of time spent on them: anything we love we spend time with, so the message any child in this situation receives is clear; and they will have felt little of serenity and peace as their childhood house was anything but the refuge a home should be. It's so tragic because your home ought to be a safe sanctuary, rather than the opposite it so often is: a battleground. It's no wonder some people spend the rest of their lives trying to cope and deal with this.

So group therapy can work for people exceptionally well, although there is something that is needed that's vital. One significant reason the 12 Steps groups are so effective, if someone truly wants what's freely on offer, is that there is most nearly always enough people in the group who have walked the journey of spiritual awakening by doing the 12 Steps and reading the accompanying literature and consistently going regularly to plenty of 12 Steps group meetings and listening to the wisdom on offer and regularly speaking with their sponsor – a mentor who has gone through the 12 Steps and someone who is a caring listener.

These more experienced people, or "old-timers" as known if they have anything like several years 12 Steps sobriety under their belt, can guide the group. Frequently this is done indirectly to someone who may share something in which they, clearly to the more experienced and the old-timers there, need some guidance. So, for instance, an old-timer may address the solution when it's their turn to talk to the group by sharing their own experience of it. We all struggle with the same. There is always a solution.

Every hero needs at least one mentor. "Sharing" is the word used for when a person in the 12 Steps group speaks to the rest of the group for five or so minutes, more or less, depending on the size of the group and duration of the meeting. It is encouraged in sharing to speak about your, as it says in the 12 Steps literature: "experience, strength and hope" and to always speak with mind of anyone new (the "newcomer") at the meeting as well as anyone there who could be struggling.

Most usually this is not done directly to the people concerned as it allows that person to make any realisation themselves, and an inner realisation is what is needed: the best teachers are those who show you were to look, but don't tell you what to see. This is the role that sponsors play and others who share well. Great Love never intervenes unless it's invited. People needing guidance will also not usually be directly referred to in the meeting – although casual one-on-one chats normally take place after the meetings – as this may put them on the spot, which is hard if self-esteem is low.

"Esteem", meaning "the regard in which one is held" – with "regard" coming from words meaning "to look" – derives from Middle English estemen meaning "to estimate", from Anglo-French estimer, from Latin aestimare. Then "self-esteem" really means: how do you look at and value yourself? If that is low it is not a great place to be and more often than not it's a terrible place. So to boost self-esteem, to increase how you value yourself it's necessary to do estimable things, priceless things, be valuable to people, do loving things for them that have no price tag on. Be like this every day and you will soon value yourself: the human condition is one that's been created to feel more value inside when we think of and show kindness to others. It's a design for life and it really works.

Group therapy gives an opportunity for this. But it is vital that there are experienced people who have their lives on track that are guiding the group. Otherwise, and this is a particular risk in rehab centres, it is like sitting the people together in just another dysfunctional family. Sickness begets sickness, hurt people hurt people. Many hard-drinking pubs will be an example of this unwell form of group therapy, as will gangs of different kinds. The people here are looking for a family, to satisfy a human need. They are looking for love and acceptance and approval for who they are. But they don't yet know who they are, how strong and beautiful they are, for who they are presently is shaped by a failure of love – so they form postures to fit in with the gangs or in the pubs or in the business or political communities.

They are just trying to lose that inner voice, the adversary within plotting against, that says they're worthless. Money often becomes a goal, because it is worth something, but this is not the sort of worth they are really needing to find. This is not the real worth that humans were designed to discover. Those people are frequently just digging the hole deeper, and further down into the darker.

As Mitch Albom wrote in the words of his mentor Morrie Schwartz in Tuesdays With Morrie. "Money is not a substitute for tenderness, and power is not a substitute for tenderness. I can tell you, as I'm sitting here dying, when you most need it, neither money nor power will give you the feeling you're looking for, no matter how much of them you have."

Considering we have this mental capacity inside us anyway, to be so condemning, it really does not help if a parent or caregiver of some sort was persistently critical – and many people report how their stifling voice inside has the same accent and tone as one or both of their parents or a main adult carer in life as they grew up. I met a man once in his mid-30s who didn't think he could read very well. He could read as well as anyone, but a scathing comment from a teacher when he was aged eight had loudly rattled around in him for decades. With a little encouragement and a change in belief, he has since gone on to read aloud hundreds of times including in front of dozens of people at 12 Steps groups, allowing him over the 17 years of his 12 Steps sobriety to help thousands of people.

So you can say, okay, I'm stuck in a hole. Then you can either carry on digging and look around and focus on all the possible ways that you think there are to not get out of it; or you can be a different sort of realistic about it, look around and go maybe it's not as bad as I was thinking, I am here now but that doesn't mean I'll be here forever, there must be a way out. You can always search for people who have been there and got out of that hole or a very similar hole. Ask them how they did it. Anyone who's been down there is more likely to be able to tell you, and with enthusiasm, because they will say: "I know what it's like down there, how dark and despairing it is, but I also know what it's like when you get out of there." All these choices are yours.

There may be two people stuck down a hole and for certain the one by far most likely to get out is the one who's looking on the positive side, who's not using up all their energy with negative thoughts that are going nowhere except deeper into the endless abyss, further into that formless void, with only darkness covering them. If you don't face something it will grow: that darkness gets darker, and that abyss gets larger, deeper; and you shrink and then you will completely disappear from sight. Instead, focus on the light and the fresh air and the sunshine and getting out and knowing that you have the courage to do that.

"And the light shines in darkness, and the darkness comprehended it not." (John 1 in the Bible.)

We need to make friends with and know that our thoughts can be our friends. Many people make this shift by doing such as daily positive affirmations or gratitude lists. A very advantageous way to do this is with a pen and paper, write down just before bedtime ten things for which you are grateful: this can be big things such as your health, your five senses, your friends, running water, food to eat, nature, a place to sleep, every breath you take; and it can be smaller things (but that are also all too often taken for granted) such as shoes to wear, hair dye, books, the internet, your favourite TV programme, coffee… (I know, maybe coffee is a big thing!) In the morning, soon after you wake up – and ideally after 30 minutes of prayer and meditation or include it in this – read through your gratitude list. You will find that depression and anxiety cannot co-exist alongside gratitude. If during the day you find yourself drifting into worry and melancholy again, read the list again or write a new one. Repeat this medicine as needed. It will help direct your thinking to positive pathways.

A prayer that many in 12-Step recovery say in the mornings goes like this: God, direct my thinking today so that it be rid of self-pity, dishonesty, self-will, self-seeking and fear. Inspire my thinking, decisions and intuitions. Help me to relax and take it easy. Free me from doubt and indecision. Guide me through this day and show me my next step. Give me what I need to take care of any problems. I ask all these things that I may be of maximum service to you and my fellow man in the name of the Steps I pray. Amen.

Notice that it says nothing about stopping the addiction such as drinking, but it's all really about feelings and thinking. It's why many in recovery from alcoholism say such as "I don't have a drinking problem, I have a thinking problem!"

Prayer comes from Latin precarius, and simply means to "obtain by entreaty" and "entreaty" means "an earnest or humble request". I like to think of it as exactly that and to realise that if I don't ask, then maybe the Universe, Higher Power, God, Mother Nature, doesn't really know that's what I'd like – in much the same way if one of my children doesn't say at the breakfast table that they would like to visit the beach that day, I don't know that. If they ask for that though, then if we can, we will go. I also realise that some of my requests may not be met because they are not good for me or the world around me. So, if one of my children asks for a powerful motorbike for instance, however much they plead and however loving and beautiful they are (as they are!), I'm not going to give that as I know they cannot ride a motorbike, so it's all too possible they could have an accident that could hurt them and hurt others too.

You can believe that every thought is a prayer. It's what religious texts were telling us centuries ago. As it was written in the Bible: "And all things, whatsoever you shall ask in prayer, believing, you shall receive."

Then Shakespeare in Hamlet wrote: "My words fly up, My thoughts remain below: Words without thoughts never to heaven go."

Ask, believe, receive.

It's the law of attraction. It is what the bestselling book The Secret by Rhonda Byrne was about: that thoughts can change a person's life directly. Acknowledged in The Secret is The Power Of Positive Thinking by minister Norman Vincent Peale that was published in 1952 and was on to this too. Peale's suggestions included: Picture yourself as succeeding. Think a positive thought to drown out a negative thought. Do not attempt to copy others. Repeat "If God be for us, who can be against us?" ten times every day. Work with a counsellor. Develop a strong self-respect. Believe that you receive power from God.

What about this "power from God"? You might strongly say you don't believe in God. This is addressed in the Big Book with a chapter titled We Agnostics, of which one part says: "Our human resources, as marshalled by the will, were not sufficient; they failed utterly. Lack of power, that was our dilemma. We had to find a power by which we could live, and it had to be a Power greater than ourselves… But where and how were we to find this Power? Well, that's exactly what this book is about.

Its main object is to enable you to find a Power greater than yourself which will solve your problem."

In that same book, the chapter called The Doctor's Opinion – written by Dr William Silkworth who'd treated more than 40,000 alcoholics and was regarded as one of the world's leading experts in the field – also says the same: "… unless this person can experience an entire psychic change, there is very little hope of his recovery. … One feels that something more than human power is needed to produce the essential psychic change."

So it's about having a psychic change and finding a greater power to deal with any personal powerlessness over an addiction or other mental health condition. This book, as with the Big Book, will help you to do that by helping you through the 12 Steps, atheist or agnostic or strong believer in God alike.

Daily meditation helps immensely as well with all of this, as can (and it seems obvious but is often not considered) reading and watching positive stuff. Choose supportive and positive friends who generally live in solutions not problems; and if your family is critical and negative, keep your time with them to a limit, and prepare yourself for it, forgive them and before and after contact do such as meditation, positive affirmations and gratitude lists. Try not to fall into the family trait of negativity and criticism by seeing if you can include something about each family person you spent some time with on your gratitude list. If you spend time after being with people like this criticising them for being so negative, being negative about their criticism… it's just the same.

It might take time, training you might call it, especially if you grew up in a negative house that taught you to focus on the lack and the negative and to be a constant critic, in an environment where the first question to any idea was always some form of: "But let's think of everything that can go wrong with that then…" It can be done, start with that loving thought: "I can do this." Start with a statement that is some form of: "Let's think of everything that can go right with that then…" If you become friends with your mind it will undoubtedly empower you.

Think how we even say: "I dream that I can do…" this or that. Dreams are thoughts... unconscious ones. We seem to have no choice during the night of whether they are something we don't want to awaken from or a nightmare. During daylight hours, we do have the choice though, so always choose dreams over nightmares.

A mental picture or a dream of sorts always has to come before there's any brilliant achievement. Know that there's a greater force around that knows your qualities and skills, because they were given to you that way. Think big with your dream, to ensure you reach the stars. It really needs to be something that has integrity and helps others. Then it will attract other people and resources and be something that lasts, possibly even beyond your lifetime.

As happens in our minds with our dreams when sleeping and awake, Campbell wrote about symbols of mythology that they: "are not manufactured; they cannot be ordered, invented, or permanently suppressed. They are spontaneous productions of the psyche… And they are in fact the vehicles of communication between the deeper depths of our spiritual life and this relatively thin layer of consciousness by which we govern our daylight existences."

So myths and Hero's Journey stories are manifestations of the deepest layers of the unconscious that reveal eternal truths about yearnings and fears and hopes of every person who has ever lived, who is alive, and who will ever live. They reveal the very nature of the human soul. As do the 12 Steps. They are all models to help spiritual and psychological growth that makes the unconscious conscious. That's why this all has some mysterious stirring inside of a familiar connection to past lives. It's a quite beautiful feeling, but can also seem overwhelming, even unsettling. It's like when we are falling in love. Maybe we are. With the Oneness.

It's also akin to creativity: anyone who writes or makes films or music or art of any kind knows how it develops on its own, certainly the best stuff comes that way, that which we say is divinely inspired. It's as if something else is the author, editor or director; almost as if there's been a dialogue between the unconscious and the conscious. It's why such creations outlive us all and even if from centuries ago are still immensely relevant today. They are symbolistic communication that speaks from the spirit directly to our souls inside. Civilisations are born and based on these, including our own modern-day societies.

M Scott Peck wrote in The Road Less Traveled about how he thought addiction and in fact all mental illness was caused when the gap between our conscious will and our unconscious will becomes too far apart – the unconscious will being our ego and the unconscious will being God's will. He wrote: "It is because our conscious self resists our unconscious wisdom that we become ill."

Peck explained how his task as a psychiatrist was always to bring these two back together as close as possible. Revealingly, the word "psychiatrist", a word first used 200 years ago, derives from Greek psukhe "soul" and iatros meaning "healer", so psychiatrist actually originally means "soul healer". Psukhe was also used to mean "breath".

Jordan Peterson has brilliantly said, describing what Jung wrote in his Red Book: "We embody a lot of information in our action. Our action has developed as a consequence of imitating other people, not only those around us, but the people before us imitated those before them and those people imitated those before them and so on, as far back as you can go. So you embody these patterns of behaviour. They are extremely informative, that you don't understand, that are the consequence of collective imitation across the centuries. Then those patterns can become manifest as figures of the imagination. And those figures of the imagination are the distillations of patterns of behaviour. And so, as the distillations of patterns of behaviour, they have content, but it's not you, that content. You can even think of it as content that's evolved – although it's actually culturally transmitted – and so these figures of the imagination can reveal the structure of reality to you."

The figures of the imagination in the myths and Hero's Journey stories, as with the 12 Steps, are about enabling us to live as confident human beings, perhaps especially when we are put in a position where we are facing chaos. It's about understanding our own place in the universe.

Written at some point from the 5th to the 2nd Century BC, the Bhagavad Gita ("Song of God") 700-verse Hindu scripture, teaches this with immortal messages such as:

- Being your best ideal is the reward in itself.
- Nothing is permanent so we have to accept changes in life.
- The soul never dies and so a fearless soul has nothing to worry about, including death.

- Nothing in this world belongs to us, everything belongs to God and we are taking nothing material with us when we die.
- Everything that happens, it happens for a reason.
- Anger, greed and lust will put us in hell.

Everyone will experience problems and dilemmas in life: chaos. The Bhagavad Gita has a major scene where there is utter confusion on the battlefield as main character Arjun is faced with a dilemma of whether to fight against (and aim to kill) people he knows. Here Krishna – the most important earthly incarnation of Vishnu, the supreme deity of Hindus – becomes Arjun's mentor. Krishna empowers Arjun to make his own choices, and the story is about getting us all to realise we have more power than we think, that we are more powerful than anything we are going through, that the problems and dilemmas, confusions and challenges, that we all have throughout life are smaller than us. We can always overcome, and we have the total energy within us to make a difference.

It's like the phrase "I will handle it" that is in Susan Jeffers' Feel The Fear And Do It Anyway; it's as Matt Haig wrote in Reasons To Stay Alive: "Depression is also smaller than you. Always, it is smaller than you, even when it feels vast. It operates within you, you do not operate within it. It may be a dark cloud passing across the sky but – if that is the metaphor – you are the sky. You were there before it. And the cloud can't exist without the sky, but the sky can exist without the cloud."

Incidentally, many of the most popular self-help books, including Reasons To Stay Alive and such as John Bradshaw's Healing The Shame That Binds You; Codependent No More by Melody Beattie; Wayne Dyer's Your Erroneous Zones; Eckhart Tolle's The Power Of Now; and You Can Heal your Life by Louise Hay to name a few, are at least in part Hero's Journey stories, written by people who have found the hero inside by confronting the chaos of their greatest fears.

Vishnu or a Higher Power or God, whatever you want to call this, can always be your mentor as well as someone who is mortal. So with the 12 Steps it is suggested to always keep a sponsor to sound out anything you consider is divine guidance. This is something anyone on a spiritual journey is advised to do, to speak with someone else further along the spiritual journey. The Bhagavad Gita explains how the seasons change, but that we must accept and tolerate and be patient with life's ups and downs, our warm light summers and our harsh dark winters, without ever losing the focus on what is our main purpose. Those who have become willing to depend upon a Higher Power, a God as you understand God, will tell how it's really a means of gaining true independence of the spirit.

The more dependent we are on a Greater Power, the more independent we will be. In the Twelve

Steps And Twelve Traditions it states: "Our whole trouble had been the misuse of willpower. We had tried to bombard our problems with it instead of attempting to bring it into agreement with God's intention for us."

Like this, going on the Hero's Journey means going beyond ourselves to something that gives and reveals to us a Greater Power. This is revealed through personal agonies as in the Bhagavad Gita, the Bible, the myths, and many bestsellers and Hollywood films that follow this pattern. They speak of the struggles caused by attachment to material things as well as emotions, and the importance of pursuing Truth. (That's another way of spelling Love.)

This can be clearly seen when spiritual teacher and writer Eckhart Tolle describes the "inner transformation" he experienced one night in 1977, aged 29, after having suffered from long periods of depression. He describes how he was awakened from his sleep, suffering from depressive feelings that were "almost unbearable" – but how he then experienced a life-changing epiphany: "I couldn't live with myself any longer. And in this a question arose without an answer: who is the 'I' that cannot live with the self? What is the self? I felt drawn into a void! I didn't know at the time that what really happened was the mind-made self, with its heaviness, its problems, that lives between the unsatisfying past and the fearful future, collapsed. It dissolved. The next morning I woke up and everything was so peaceful. The peace was there because there was no self. Just a sense of presence or 'beingness', just observing and watching."

It is often written that God is Love. Some may call it Mother Nature, Allah, Vishnu, the Highest Good or the Universe. The name is a name, a sound. What matters is that we know if we stand up tall and live in a certain way, Love will be revealed and as Joseph Campbell put it: "... the universe will open doors for you where there were only walls."

There is this order that is both liveable in and that has heavenliness, splendour and magnificence for us to realise. It will give real meaning to life. In Love we trust. It is the Truth.

While the theme of the hero myth is universal and has occurred in every culture in every time, it is as infinitely varied as the characters that make up the human race itself. Yet its basic form remains the same. Campbell noticed that different cultures told very similar stories of a person who left a familiar world, stepped into the unknown, confronted fear and more often than not forces of death, and in doing so discovered and then gave all of us the knowledge of how to overcome death, to have eternal life.

A hero shows us that what is worth living for and what is worth dying for are the same thing. In his book Mentors, comedian turned 12 Steps guru

Russell Brand writes: "A hero is an emblem that demonstrates the possibility of inner drives becoming manifest."

We can get closer to something like Paradise by living in the Truth, always in Love. Truth is trust, belief and faith. Unconditional love. A hero puts the Truth above their own ego. Love above all. It's a psychological death and rebirth. Sometimes the hero does even physically die as a result of putting the Truth first. Yet in doing so they pass on the Truth to others: in dying they live forever. This was the forever victory that Jesus Christ achieved.

A hero always aims for the greatest good, and so always has to speak the Truth. The suffering that's an integral part of the human condition can redeem itself through Truth. That's the answer the myths and Hero's Journey stories are telling us, responding to the question: how should we best live our life? They contain ideas that have been tried that haven't died, and so that have become known ways of living to the greatest ideal that a human being can attain.

It's very scientific: test, observe, conclude (Fact).

At some point early on in life, every human being realises that all life is under the stopwatch. We get to know the explicit history of humankind and we can see ourselves in the mirror. All too often, this is when we start to move away from the Truth of trust, belief, faith and unconditional love. The Hero's

Journey's stories are urging us to move back to that we are at the beginning. As close to Paradise as we can get.

Repeating characters seen in the hero myth, such as the young hero, the wise older mentor, the shape-shifting woman or man, and the shadowy antagonist are identical with the archetypes of our mind, as revealed in dreams. When we realise that we have no say in what we dream, we can realise their importance in revealing important things to us. Think of Christ and Satan. If you don't believe in them as real, then there can be no denying that they arose from forms created in the human mind. (And maybe that they came there from the spirit via the soul?) They came because Christ and Satan represent the extremes of humanity that hang in the balance. Humans can go to both ends of that scale.

From ultimate evil to ultimate good. Dark to light. Enemy to hero. No-love to love.

We must always better evil, resolve suffering, and make ourselves excellent and effective. On levels of evil in people: what permission do we give – to ourselves and to others? We seem to certainly have within us the capability to override that which we know that is deeper inside us to be right or wrong. That is, human beings can use something about their consciousness to become louder than their subconsciousness: ranging from dishonesty in some form, such as dressing up a bad motive as a good motive, right down to justifying genocide.

73

Myths and Hero's Journey stories strike something in us that we know to be true. Such stories are true. They are models of the workings of the human mind, real maps of the psyche and they stir our soul, they create feelings of terror and awe. They are psychologically valid and realistic even when they portray fantastic, impossible, unreal characters and events.

As an example, people throughout history before connection to other civilisations, have had some form of a dragon to defeat (although in some cultures such as China the dragon protects). Dragon comes from the Greek word drakon meaning "serpent", and it's often represented by a snake-like creature. Serpent or snake symbolism played essential parts in the cultural and religious life of ancient Egypt, Canaan, Mesopotamia and Greece. Serpents were a symbol of evil power and chaos from the underworld (as well as sometimes a symbol of life, fertility and healing). As with in the Bible, the serpent in the Garden of Eden and the sea serpent monster Leviathan. And as in the Mesopotamian Epic Of Gilgamesh, in which Gilgamesh loses the power of immortality when it is stolen by a snake.

In Mesopotamia – which roughly corresponds today to most of Iraq, Kuwait, eastern Syria, and southeastern Turkey, and where what we now know as civilisation started to form at least 16,000 years ago – a god existed who was known as Marduk, likely pronounced as "Marutuk" that shows his association with the sun god Utu. Marduk, described as having a divine radiance and often referred to as "lord", captured in a net the goddess Tiamat, a sea serpent or dragon that symbolised chaos. Tiamat had assembled an army of dragons and monsters led by the god of darkness Kingu, to whom she gave the Tablet Of Destinies – a clay tablet with a cuneiform inscription – and whoever possessed this ruled the universe.

But Marduk overcame Kingu's army and killed Tiamat with an arrow that split her into halves. With one half of her, Marduk made the heavens and then created the Earth from the other. So where we live is created from chaos... After this, Marduk killed Kingu. Mixing Kingu's blood with earth, Marduk made a clay from which was modelled the first people, created to serve the gods and take care of the Earth. Some versions say the bones of the dead dragons and monsters were also used in the creation of people.

We people were created with the blood of the god of darkness, bones of monsters and live on some part of chaos. That doesn't sound very pleasant! But it was acknowledging and explaining that disorder we see around us to varying degrees as well as the shadow side inside all of us. The shadow side is the portion of the personality that has all the parts of ourselves that we don't want to admit to having. Jung thought the shadow side was the uncivilised, primitive side of our nature. He was convinced we needed to realise and face our shadow to become more complete and balanced. This is because just because we repress aspects of ourselves, they do not disappear. Instead, they can grow in the dark and cause burgeoning difficulties as they increasingly take hold of us.

The name Devil comes from Greek diabolos meaning "slanderer". It is clear at times that our insanity comes from within, we are under attack from the enemy within, the darkness is running in our blood. We even say about someone who is behaving erratically: "What the hell has got into them?" or about ourselves: "I really can't explain what got into me." A dark shadow is hidden inside us then, but we have to confront it to defeat it. If we are standing on order created from chaos, and change is inevitable as it is… then we must be ready and best prepared, which is something the myths and Hero's Journey stories and 12 Steps teach us how to be.

Why would human beings have a shadow side? Because the entire world is made of opposites, yin and yang: yin originally referred to the shady side of a slope while yang referred to the sunny side – there are always complementary and opposing characteristics in nature, such as sky and earth, day and night, water and fire, active and passive, male and female. Chaos and order. The shadow side may be complex, but maybe what matters most is not to deny it. Because we can deceive ourselves.

From the Book Of Revelation in the Bible it says:
"And the great dragon was cast out, that old
serpent, called the Devil, and Satan, which
deceiveth the whole world: he was cast out into the
earth, and his angels were cast out with him."

A hero archetype's main feat is to overcome the
dragon of darkness. Face and slay your greatest
fears – and the glorious victory gained is
fearlessness.

From the Israelites and Aztecs to the Aborigines
and the Norsemen to the varied cultures of Africa
and Asia, there was some form of dragon. In fact,
dragon motifs have been found on pottery that are
from before what we usually consider the dawn of
civilisation.

In ancient Egypt, Ra was the solar deity, the bringer
of light, and thus the upholder of "Ma'at" that were
the concepts of truth, balance and order. Apep was
the ancient Egyptian deity that embodied chaos as
the opponent of light, order and truth – and so was
the greatest enemy of Ra. Appearing as a giant
serpent, every day Apep hid below the horizon to
wait for Ra when the sun set. Each 24 hours saw a
battle between light and darkness. It really was "one
day at a time".

In us, the battle between Heaven and Hell takes
place in the mind. They are entities. The ego should
be the servant of the self. It's a bit like a TV aerial
bringing in all the channels from the airwaves and

giving a choice to the viewer. But through such as childhood issues or trauma the ego can disassociate from the self. It can start to run the show – using the TV analogy it will start to select only one signal, give only one channel to the viewer. The other channels are still there, but the ego has taken over. The one channel is called something like Love Me & Approve Of Me.

We have a choice over our thoughts, the 60,000 to 80,000 of them we have a day (author and alternative-medicine advocate Deepak Chopra cites this estimation when writing about why we should meditate; and 70,000 thoughts a day is a number attributed to the University of Southern California's Laboratory of Neuro Imaging). That's around 4,000 thoughts every waking hour. It seems a lot but anyone who's ever had what's termed in 12 Steps groups a "washing machine mind", especially if it's been on fast spin, might relate to this. It's one reason often cited as getting drunk or stoned: to slow down or numb out the thoughts, or to block them out if blackout is reached.

In general, your thoughts will be a mixture of negative, positive and inquisitive, depending on such as family blueprint and what environment and situation you find yourself in. But when the disassociated ego stages its takeover, it is doing so because of a failure of love in some form, most commonly trauma and/or toxic shame, and it attempts to find that lost love. But it gets selfish and self-centred at this. This creates a division between the ego and the spirit, the true self. It is exactly as the Alcoholics Anonymous book puts it: "Selfishness – self-centredness! That, we think, is the root of our troubles."

As its weapons, the disassociated ego uses such as suppression, denial and idealisation. The thoughts that then dominate create feelings that are unpleasant and these feelings create more negative thoughts, and so on spiralling downwards. Everything we focus on grows, so anxiety makes for more anxiety, depression more depression. Negative gets more negative. The black dog gets darker and bigger and louder.

Due to this failure of love, we may have instinctively hidden our soul, our real self, as best we can. We are protecting it. We do our best to hide the vulnerable little boy or girl. The inner child is sometimes hidden away so well for their protection they are never seen again...

But what are today termed mental health issues such as anxiety or depression are actually the soul's way of getting attention, an attempt at holding up a sign to where the person should be going, to how they should be living if they are living the Truth. The sign reads: "This is the route to being the person you're supposed to be (please walk this way to know meaning, fulfilment and happiness)." The damaged ego fights going in this direction though as there are other signs reading: "Family and society expectations and demands; financial traps."

Mitch Albom wrote in Tuesdays With Morrie: "Well, for one thing, the culture we have does not make people feel good about themselves. We're teaching the wrong things. And you have to be strong enough to say if the culture doesn't work, don't buy it. Create your own. Most people can't do it."

There is also fear that going in the right direction means looking at some things that this ego says need not be looked at or convinces it's too frightening to look at them. So these signs are often pointing in completely opposite directions. Then the spirit tries harder to get the person's attention, as it knows the real person in there is dying if it doesn't do so. It wants to bring that hidden child into the adult, full of love, where and how it should be. It can feel painful because birth and growth are painful – and it has to be that way to get our attention so we stay focussed.

It's just like any of us would shout to someone in the distance who was running with their eyes shut towards a great drop off a cliff edge. As they got closer to the edge we would shout louder. And louder still if they still didn't stop, until the point that we'd be shouting as loud as we could. We might even chuck a rock at them – to get their attention, to stop them in their tracks – which would bloody hurt if it hit them, but would not hurt as much or be as devastating as if they carried on until the cliff edge.

A cliff would not be most people's favoured spot to face a dragon... Surely there's enough danger with a dragon alone... But in Beowulf, the Old English epic poem, a Hero's Journey story written between 975 and 1025, king of the Goth tribe Beowulf sets out to find a dragon that has terrorised his realm. The dragon lives in a womb-like barrow by a cliff where it guards some considerable treasure. It is the earliest example we know of in literature of the now typical European fire-breathing dragon and the first piece of English literature to present a dragon-slayer, although these heroic figures already existed in such as Norse sagas and Germanic literature. They had three typical narratives for the dragon-slayer: a fight for the treasure; a battle to save the slayer's people; or a fight to free a woman. These are all hugely symbolic.

Beowulf, described as being "death-ripe", finds the dragon and calls it out with "a strong-hearted bellow". His people's fate depends on the outcome of the fight with the dragon, and, as a hero, Beowulf knows he must kill the dragon or be killed. After saying he is accepting to "give up loaned time" on Earth, he bravely defeats it with the help of his younger kinsman Wiglaf, the only one of his tribe who came to help him against the ferocious dragon. Beowulf is mortally wounded in the battle after getting poisoned by the dragon's fangs, and before he dies he nominates Wiglaf as his heir. The dead dragon is later pushed off the cliff into the sea. Beowulf's body is buried in a mound that's filled with the treasure he gained from slaying the dragon.

Dragons represent everything we don't think we can ever face and overcome. For a start, they are huge and live in vast dark fathom-esque caves or cave-like places, from where they keep a stealthy watch. Some dragons never sleep. Many only come out in the darkness of the night to hunt, and they have ravenous appetites.

They have been created from the minds of humankind in every way to be the most formidable creature we could possibly imagine, for they represent our final most terrifying fears. This is why dragons are serpent-like creatures with a reptilian head yet that is also like a hound with the sharpest jagged teeth imaginable – some dragons have been known to have teeth that could become soldiers when planted in the ground. In any case, these giant sharp teeth are capable of ripping us apart alive and leaving us in pieces to die (sometimes slowly in agonising pain) – all very significant as this is what our largest fears when not confronted feel to do to us: they tear us apart and leave us scattered all over the place.

It's how in one of the Egyptian myths, Osiris the god of fertility, resurrection and life, is killed by Set who was god of chaos, fire, trickery, storms, envy, disorder and violence – and frequently considered to be the forebear of the concept of Satan. Set dismembered Osiris's body into more than 40 pieces and flung them across Egypt.

Dragons of course notoriously breathe fire, so hot they can melt swords or other weapons we may bring for them. The scorching fire, symbolic of hellfire, makes the air so hot and dry that it scorches the inside of our throats so that we are left speechless. The shooting flames burn the oxygen so we can barely breathe and gasp for each breath, terrified that we are bound to die. Its fire and searing heat from them shoot out so far we dare not even consider at times that we can approach the dragon without feeling that scorching pain and getting turned to ash. That is even if we could see anything to make our way through the acrid smell and dense fogginess caused by their smoke-snorting nostrils. It is as if we are blinded and with a muddled mind.

A dragon has blood-red eyes that pierce into us even if we can find the bravery to look at them. Their look alone has been known to turn people to stone. The overall reptilian look of a dragon sinks deeply into our own reptilian brain, the oldest part that controls the body's vital functions such as heart rate, breathing, body temperature and balance. They fluctuate wildly. Fight or flight. Or freeze, which is like being turned to stone.

A dragon's roar – forked tongue protruding, because they only ever deceive – can cause vibrations that shake the earth, stopping us from going a step closer unless we use every part of our will and might. We have to really want to reach them.

Yet even if we got close enough to confront the dragon, it has devil-like horns on its head, sharp as swords. Some dragons have more than one head as well. The dragon's skin appears impenetrable. What could possibly pierce it? And even if we did, dragon's blood has been known to be acidic to scorch into us and burn us to an agonising slow death. Other dragons have blood that's poison.

If we crept up from behind, it has a powerful tail lined with spikes that would kill us with one blow or impale us and fling us around at will. The tail is pointed so that it can stab us to death too.

Then the dragon has giant bat-like wings, these too adorned with lethal spikes. It can fly and swoop at will like an enormous eagle at its prey. Think of the Hungarian Horntail in Harry Potter. It can cast inescapable shadows over us, clouds of stormy darkness, and seize us whenever it wants. On its giant paw-like or eagle-feet, huge enough alone to pound us to death, are claws that could clearly shred our skin to pieces with just one swipe or that could grasp us away and off into the sky. With its muscular legs it can run as fast as anything on land, moving it at a pace that nothing can run away from, from which nothing on Earth can escape.

No wonder it seems to many like the easier option is to keep on drinking excessively, smoking dope, working too much, busying ourselves with anything that doesn't really need doing, eating too much too often, taking the tablets, obsessing over sex, putting on another bet – or whatever the equivalent is in each individual person... But what when you know those large flaring nostrils have smelt you, that those blood-red eyes are definitely on you? What then, what then?

So the Greek word drakon means "serpent" and that word is derived from the Greek verb "derkomai", meaning "I see". A dragon and what it is capable of is greatly symbolic of the human emotions such as anxiety and panic attacks that leave us gasping for our life-giving oxygen; or that we are frozen in fear. Or that our depression has turned us to stone; stress is scorching our skin; or that an addiction has impaled us and is flinging us around at will and ripping us to pieces and scattering our dismembered parts all over the place but not actually finally killing us, yet.

Suffering is an integral part of the human condition. Chaos is close to order, and vice versa, the path of the moral code or corruption is where we walk every second, making choices whether we go on the straight path or stray from it. For the majority of people, even when shown the way, they won't take it. It remains the road less travelled. They don't know and can't see where the Yellow Brick Road goes. So they just stay stuck at the dead end in Kansas, kind of already dead.

In fact, it can be seen that the Yellow Brick Road symbolises the way anyone can purify their soul while advancing spiritually, such as in Buddhism and Taoism; the way the soul is guided in order to return home.

"When I let go of what I am, I become what I might be," said Lao Tzu, philosopher and founder of Taoism who is thought to have lived in the 6th to 4th Century BC. The Tao means "the way", and can be thought of as the flow of the universe, that there's an essence behind the natural world that keeps the universe balanced and in order. This force, the Tao, in the universe is greater, higher, deeper and more true than any other force. It's usually described in terms of elements of nature, and especially as similar to water: like water it is uniform, eternally self-replenishing, soft and quiet, yet also immensely powerful and impassively generous. The philosophy of yin and yang is where such as water flowing gently in a river is yin and rushing over the waterfall it is yang. The way to live is in harmony with the Tao – go with the flow, live simply and with compassion.

In a Hero's Journey sense it is most like Star Wars creator George Lucas said of the Force having two sides. "It is not a malevolent or a benevolent thing. It has a bad side to it, involving hate and fear; and it has a good side, involving love, charity, fairness and hope. If you use it well, you can see the future and the past."

Lucas explained that with the Force he wanted to "awaken a certain kind of spirituality". It has been said he used the Force to "echo" its use by filmmaker Roman Kroitor in the short 1963 film 21-

87, in which Kroitor insists, while in discussion with someone claiming living beings are nothing but highly complex machines: "Many people feel that in the contemplation of nature and in communication with other living things, they become aware of some kind of force, or something, behind this apparent mask which we see in front of us, and they call it God."

So there is good and bad, although Tao is not saying there is necessarily good versus evil as in many other spiritual beliefs, such as God against Satan. But any way, there are good and bad forces – and we choose how we go with them.

It's all so connected. The myths and the Hero's Journey stories and the "religious" texts and 12 Steps literature all basically say one thing because there is only one thing to say. That is, close to, if you live life by the Greater Power of love you will know a greater power that is Love.

In John Milton's 17th Century epic poem Paradise Lost this was portrayed as a choice between obedience or disobedience to God, with Milton suggesting that the order of the world depends on humankind's obedience to God. Then that we have free will because God wants all of us to obey God out of love, not because we've been forced to do so. Satan's children Sin and Death build a bridge linking Hell and Earth. We have a choice at every second, that is both our burden and our freedom.

It was also laid out by CS Lewis in his Mere Christianity book: "If a thing is free to be good it is also free to be bad. And free will is what has made evil possible. Why, then, did God give them free will? Because free will, though it makes evil possible, is also the only thing that makes possible any love or goodness or joy worth having. A world of automata – of creatures that worked like machines – would hardly be worth creating."

So from our own consciousness we need to make this choice. It is merely a return to how we were born, before self-consciousness made life a perpetual struggle lived in the head rather than from the heart.

Poet James Kavanaugh put this fall into headlong disobedience so beautifully:
"When did you lose your eyes and ears, when did taste
Buds cease to tremble;
Whence this sullenness, this mounting fear, this quarrel
With life – demanding meaning?"

We are souls put into bodies that no one else can take hold of to relieve the physical, emotional and spiritual pain we feel. This can be due to society and family and our seeking to be enough, to justify and know why we are here, to gain approval for who we are; and no one can possibly achieve that all the time for all their life. Most people live with a sense they could be doing more, that they should have a greater responsibility to their own life, and a knowing that this would also help others more. You are strong enough to do it, but you won't know that until you do it.

Then, we reach that point in life when we are in a body that starts to disintegrate before our very eyes. We see our withering and before then we see that of such as our parents or other loved ones. It is clear that our living is also a dying. We have to be heroic to face all of this well, with any candour.

Even before then, we have a realisation of our mortality. Something pretty bloody big, like everything and it all, is out of our hands. We can exercise and eat well and meditate and not get stressed and all that will help, to a degree, but still the reality exists that one day we will die. With our current levels of consciousness, what happens to us then we cannot completely say, but as we are now will be dead, and all those with us now will be dead too. Why the hell some people kill each other then seems a bit ridiculous. Maybe we need each other and that's why we have our lives together at this time, this little moment in the 300,000 years or so of Homo sapiens.

People like us used to live in caves. One day the food source around the cave might disappear. Everyone gets hungry. Starving now. Someone has to go beyond the territorial boundaries, to boldly go where no one has gone before… They leave a normal world for an extraordinary world. When they return with something to eat they are lauded, for the food, yes, but then also for something else, something forever, for they now have gained the quality of fearlessness, and the only way to get that was to be fearless, as they were. Now they can also pass this on.

Hero's Journey stories have an appeal strongly felt by everyone because they spring from a universal source in the collective unconscious, because they reflect our universal concerns. They are the key to life. "Each person is at each moment capable of remembering all that has ever happened to him and of perceiving everything that is happening everywhere in the universe," wrote Aldous Huxley in The Doors Of Perception.

A Hero's Journey normally has 12 stages that mostly run in the same order. As manifestations of our subconscious, the hero's myth though is flexible, capable of some variation without giving up its power. The values of the story are what's important: these will outlive us all. There are, however, some key stages that someone must go through for the enlightening transformation to take place, to become heroic.

The 12 Steps are set as they are, the only exception being that frequently Step 10 is started at the same time as Step 4 because Step 4 deals with past events – resentments and secrets kept inside – and Step 10 deals in the same way with the same things but for anything that happens in the present: so for doing the 12 Steps it makes sense to start Step 4 and Step 10 written lists at the same time.

You need a sponsor, or someone who's walked the 12 Steps before you if you will. Trying it alone I think will lead to nowhere that you want to go, maybe even to heartache and more pain and tragedy. You need a guide to reach the sunny uplands, someone who knows the way. Because that way up is fraught with places to slip and fall. You need a guide like Dante had when going through Hell, you need a guide like he had in Virgil, someone who already knows the territory, someone with knowledge of these matters, a person with reason and wisdom, someone who can protect you if the devil steps in to try to lead you, someone who can fight for you if you come under attack. Dante writes of Virgil: "You are my teacher and my author."

Doing the 12 Steps alone is like trying to bite your own teeth, clap with one hand, like attempting to find a lost torch in the dark without the help of someone stood next to you with the same torch as the one you've lost. It's trying to solve the problem with the problem, to heal a flesh wound by poking it with eyes shut and then rubbing dirt in it. What you need is someone there to help you mop up the blood, to enable you to clean the wound, and then to help you put the cover on it that will allow it to heal. You need help – and even the asking of help is part of the process as it is ego-reducing humility in itself.

Humility is not to be confused with humiliation – even though humiliation in life might enable someone to develop enough humility to ask for help. Humility is about having your feet firmly planted on the ground, to remember your roots. It is about honesty, having enough responsibility and courage to truthfully look at yourself and humbly accept what you find. It is to accept yourself, and then it is to realise there is much more to you, inside you and about you, than you ever could have known by attempting it alone.

This is a broad path, a wide highway – but along the journey there are certain points that must be passed to reach the point where you become spiritually awoken and a hero.

It shows you how to not be afraid or discouraged, how to be strong and courageous. The problem for many in our modern society, that leads to apathy or depression, is that what society and family expects, what that pushes us into is all too often not us. We know that, the gut feeling, our soul lets us know, and so we prefer to stay in bed doing nothing, or drink too much, smoke too much, anything to distract and avoid – because we'd rather do nothing much useful than set off in or continue in what we know to be the wrong direction.

So this is one reason for such as the depression, the aimlessness, the feeling of general apathy and hopelessness: the acedia. But this is why they are all signposts for us to look to because they read

Definitely Not That Way. Too many people ignore that signpost, then reach the end of their life and, despite any seeming successes, they realise they've lived the wrong life... Can you imagine?

You need to ask: what is my true purpose? Consider your talents and know not to be fearful of using and sharing them. They were given to you for an amazing reason, a very special reason. Don't compare yourself to others. You are created entirely individually. There's no one else around right now who can play your role.

Perhaps there is someone who can help you: seek out those people, the ones who are encouraging and enthusing. Be among the people who help you to discover your talents and abilities, then to nurture and utilise them, be among those who are keen for you to thrive. Be one of these people to others too.

This poem, it's for everyone: "Courageous girl, You may be terrified to your very core, but make sure you do it anyway. I promise you, that moment of courage will change your life. It will open doors, whether it's the door you want or another door that's meant for you. It will push you forward into something more than what was before."

There's a parable in the Bible told by Jesus that's quite brilliant and completely relevant today – it's from this parable that our present meaning of "talent" derives from: "having a natural skill." It is about a master who has three servants and as he has to go away for a while he gives them each a "talent" to look after, a talent then being a unit of currency worth a significant amount.

When this master eventually returns he asks his three servants what they have done with the talents he had given them. The first two servants step up and tell him they have used their talents, and consequently doubled their value. The master is so pleased he rewards them.

Then the remaining servant says that because he knows the master is a hard man he had buried his talent, because he was afraid. The master is furious and calls him lazy, and says that he could have at least just taken it to the bank to make some money from it. He takes the talent from him and gives it to the others. This is where the often misunderstood biblical phrase arises: "For whoever has will be given more, and they will have an abundance. Whoever does not have, even what they have will be taken from them."

We need to live to our full God-given potential using the talents we've been given. Maybe consider that it could be seen as selfish not to, like keeping a great gift to yourself or just burying it away rather than letting the world be better because of it. If you don't use your gifts, then you will surely feel it. It won't feel good, because your inside will be desperately trying to get your attention to tell you that your outside is going in the wrong direction or is in the wrong place for you. When your inside matches your outside you will know it, and it feels flawless. Those who are fearless know this.

This book is an interpretation showing the phenomenal parallels between the 12 Steps and the Hero's Journey. How they connect is an open evaluation. What's certain is that the 12 Steps take you on an amazing Hero's Journey that lets everyone who goes on it find the real hero inside.

1. Always be rigorously honest to yourself and others

Step 1 of the 12 Steps: We admitted we were powerless over alcohol [or our addiction, gambling, our emotions, food etc] – that our lives had become unmanageable.

"What makes a king out of a slave? Courage!" says the Cowardly Lion in The Wizard Of Oz.

That's where this journey starts, with the courage to be honest with ourselves. No more denial. As the recovery joke goes: "Denial is not a river in Egypt..." So before we begin, at the thought of taking the first step, we have to be honest – this above all: to thine own self be true.

To answer this question, you only have to feel down into your heart and sense what your gut is saying. Are you happy, do you feel a missing part (or missing everything) down there? A gaping aching gap?

If something is amiss, welcome to humanity – it's how we've been left, and it is what all the world's religious texts have been trying to tell us across the centuries, and then offering a solution. That solution is there, but sometimes lost to many people in all the observance and dogma and profane power-striving. Anyway, so many are like teenagers as to their parents when it comes to admitting that our life is not truly our life, that there is something else other than ourselves that has a fundamental sway over us... Certainly I rebelled over that, all of that, for many years. We do rebel, perhaps the majority of us – and of course we do!

So we go it alone. Then at some point, and we've known it for a long while, we are in a grey world. This grey world means we are a lesser version of ourselves. And we know it, whatever the status or salary. We know it. We know there's something more, something much more to life. We feel unfulfilled. Deep down we know the answer to the question: is this it?

"If the doors of perception were cleansed every thing would appear to man as it is, Infinite. For man has closed himself up, till he sees all things thro' narrow chinks of his cavern," wrote William Blake in The Marriage Of Heaven And Hell. It is feasible to realise that perhaps we – humanity – actually knew more about all of this until some time starting in perhaps the 1950s.

In the 12 Steps, the first Step is an admission of powerlessness as the first step in liberation. Yet every instinct in a person cries out against this idea of personal powerlessness. Rebellion is rife!

Yet this is surrendering to win. An admission of personal powerlessness turns out to be as the AA book Twelve Steps And Twelve Traditions puts it: "firm bedrock upon which happy and purposeful lives may be built."

There has to be the emphatic realisation that at present the person is powerless over their life. In mental health terms that can be anything, whether it is depression, anxiety, OCD, trauma, alcoholism or another addiction or any other mental health condition: anything that has power over us means we are powerless over it.

If we had power over it, it wouldn't be a problem.

Anyone who is at this point then, they have to admit their hopelessness, that they are on a road to nowhere, a fatal progression. But this should be a cause for optimism, hope at admitting hopelessness, as at least there is a knowing that to continue that way will lead only to a dead end. Some may still want to make yet another attempt to carry on down that road, but that is to be thinking you are alone in this world, to deny that we are all intricately linked, to reject that you were given the gift of life for a purpose.

There has to be. No one creates something for it to be useless. Even those artists who have made something that may appear that way at first glance have done so with the thought of usefulness behind the creation. Take My Bed, a work by artist Tracey

Emin created in 1998, consisting of an unmade bed with what looked like various random objects strewn next to it on a blue rug. Critics sneered and called it a farce, claiming anyone could exhibit an unmade bed. To these claims the artist retorted: "Well, they didn't, did they? No one had ever done that before." She revealed the idea for My Bed was inspired by a depressive phase in her life when she'd stayed in bed for four days without eating or drinking anything but alcohol. When she looked at the mess that had gathered in her bedroom, she realised what she'd created. My Bed sold at auction for £2.5 million in 2014.

So this sort of honesty in admitting hopelessness – that we have run out of ideas, that we need help, that we are bankrupt – takes great courage. It takes great courage as we live in a society that seems to increasingly tell us to go it alone. Our schools don't yet have lessons in Going With Your Gut Instincts or Humility or Spiritual Growth. These are subjects that would help immensely in the navigation of life on life's terms.

So it takes something. We are all broken to an extent such is the nature of humanity, but so many of us hide behind masks of composure and/or status. Psychiatrist M Scott Peck wrote about this and called alcoholism the "sacred disease" because "the great blessing of alcoholism is the nature of the disease. It puts people into a visible crisis..." It is obvious that alcoholics are messing up. Even so, the majority, as with all addicts, will not get the help they need. After suffering for many years, they will die as addicts. Most will be tragically alone.

Consider the word "crisis" here: from Greek krisis meaning "act of separating, sudden change, decision, judgement, turning point" and that's from a variant stem of krinein meaning "to separate, choose, decide" – so how do we choose to view the (frequently sudden) changes that will happen in life on life's terms? Does the alcoholic, for instance, who ends up in prison due to their drinking and corrupt way of survival see this as the final end or the new beginning? Thank God, some do choose the right way to go at this crisis, this turning point, and I've met several people who have turned their life around as a result of ending up in jail. This could be anyone's choice.

In the Twelve Steps And Twelve Traditions it is written: "Under the lash of alcoholism, we are driven to AA, and there we discover the fatal nature of our situation. Then, and only then, do we become open-minded to conviction and as willing to listen as the dying can be. We stand ready to do anything..."

You can you get to this point with or without being lashed by an addiction – if only you can be rigorously honest, first and foremost with yourself, and then at some point soon with another trusted person who can help you. Ask yourself and honestly answer, is my life far from satisfactory? Is it too ordinary? Is it hell?

In a Hero's Journey the potential hero goes from their ordinary world into an extraordinary world. So the story's starting point is that ordinary world. It's usually far from satisfactory. It may look respectable, but there's usually an inner hell going on. The main character may be doing what is expected of him by family, friends, society... But they know – and we can see all too clearly (as with someone with, say, a drink or drug problem) – that they are living in calamity and desolation, that there is much more to life than the life they are living.

Life is just so drab, and they are so submissive in all that drabness. They know there's something else, something brighter – there simply has to be because presently they feel dead. But they don't know where or what that something else is. At this stage, they may never have seen anywhere else.

But deep inside them, they know, every second... It's as if the spirit is crying out to them. Maybe that's exactly what it is. It's our soul inside connected to the spirit of life that tells us if we are happy or sad, if we are fulfilling our potential or not. Carl Jung depicted this perfectly in The Red Book: "My soul, where are you? Do you hear me? I speak, I call you – are you there? I have returned, I am here again. I have shaken the dust of all the lands from my feet, and I have come to you, I am with you. After long years of long wandering, I have come to you again."

So Step 1, the opening scene of this Hero's Journey, is realising and admitting that you are a lost soul and that you are dying inside. It is saying: "I am not who I am."

In the beginning of Star Wars, protagonist Luke Skywalker is seen as a bored farm worker... before he goes out into the exciting universe to fulfil his real purpose. Harry Potter lives in a grey suburban street with a family who constantly criticises him. Dorothy in The Wizard Of Oz is put down as well by her family on the farm where she lives and, as depicted in the beginning of the film, life just has no colour.

For people with addiction problems and many other mental health problems, it's similar. The world of a heroin addict or overeater or someone trapped in their house due to anxiety or depression may seem unusual to many, but to the person there it becomes their ordinary world. In it, they are just existing. Surviving day to day. Put down and kept down by their addiction or their mental disease/spiritual sickness. Life is like a suicide by instalments. They are digging a hole into darkness, and every day they are digging it deeper and deeper.

In these scenarios the ordinary world they are in cannot go on, they really know that. They reach that point. It is unsustainable. It is unmanageable. The alcoholic at this point, as the book Alcoholic Anonymous says: "will be unable to imagine life either with alcohol or without it." That is, most people know it, but it is also astonishing how many people don't realise that what they have put in place as their solution is their first problem to confront: the person drinking every evening, or smoking weed every hour, certain so-called romantic relationships, the man or woman who works so much they barely see their children awake…

All that drinking, all that weed, all that working – it's not working. It's doing you no good at all.

Frequently it is that the people in lives like this do know, but keep it buried. They are using this thing, this addiction of some sort, to avoid having to go where they most likely need to go. The person took a drink; the drink took a person.

Somewhere within them, they know that a metaphorical dragon is going to any day now pounce to slay them. They live in a perpetual state of impending doom or perpetual fear. There is internal division. The stuff may give a temporary form of relief. But even if it somehow looks like order on the outside, inside is chaos. And yet, as Jung put it: "People will do anything, no matter how absurd, to avoid facing their own souls."

It is that the conscious will and unconscious knowing are so far apart that the gap is an abyss. Which is what the word "hell" means. This abyss feels like it has no end, that it goes on forever, an infinite darkness, a pain that has no end, a chasm that can never be crossed. There seems to be no hope.

At this point, many people, tragically, end their lives. It is not because they want to end their life: they want to end the pain of their consciousness. In other words, their thoughts are killing them. The magnifying mind is on the negative, it is focussing on lack. Whatever we focus on grows, be it good or bad. This is one reason why such as addiction and many other mental health problems are progressive. (So too is recovery by the way, but more on that to come.)

Particularly in addiction, people talk of the monkey on the back, and it just doesn't seem to be possible to shake it off. What is more, that monkey is doing press-ups 24/7, it's getting stronger, its grasp becoming ever tighter. It gets heavier and heavier, making it harder to take even one step forward. Its grip begins squeezing the chest, compressing the lungs, pressing on the heart, strangling. It's a panic attack every second, getting increasingly more choking...

Negative thoughts create feelings. The feelings are toxic. The toxic feeling leads to more negative thoughts, toxic thinking. It is often a pattern of thinking and being that's been handed down from family of origin. It is all too often how they have been taught to focus, wired to think and so to feel. The toxic shame, criticism and trauma of childhood is pushing the self-destruction button.

All of these fall under the major cause of what today are called mental health issues, that are derived from spiritual sickness: that is, a failure of love. The pushing down of this inner sensing – the distraction and depressing by means of drink, drugs, work, sex or whatever else – is no longer working. It cannot and never does forever. The toxicity spreads, until it is everywhere within.

At some point nearly everyone suffering like this, if they can look back, will realise they have hidden themselves as a child to protect that vulnerable little soul. Their inner child is in a safe hiding place. A lot of recovery is about finding that inner child, reassuring and saving them, and then bringing them into the adult version of themselves. The 12 Steps allow this.

But if the soul's fire has been dampened down and concealed to protect it, the inner coldness will grow and grow until the icy shivering is unbearable. New fires are perhaps lit, and sometimes they burn high and far, but they are not the real fire of that person. That warm blazing real light is still somewhere, flickering in a cold darkness.

It is not that people get depression, it is that they are depressing something, something terribly dark and heavy. In some way, they were made to feel unlovable. But we are human and we need to be loved.

So at some point the drugs do not work any more. They only make it worse. The fire needs to be found and rekindled, to be fully alight again, to be burning brightly, glowing and sharing its warmth and light. Sometimes it's been hidden so well and for so long to protect it, the suffering person needs to really search deep-down to find it. Into the suffering, deep into the wound… into the heart of the darkness.

If this is you, then you need to ask: why the addiction, why the anxiety, why the depression? What's the trauma, the wound, the toxic shame and where was – and perhaps still is – the failure of love that encompasses all of these? I strongly recommend help from someone who's been there and knows what they are talking about to answer these questions. Someone who has come out the other side. You may know where honest-to-goodness help is, you may have been to see the understanding and knowledgable counsellor or to the 12-Step meeting. Now you meet a certain someone or read something or see a sign…

The pain of mental health disease is to attract your attention to all of this. For all this disturbance is signposting the way to the solution for you. If not dealt with, run directly into, the pain will only ever get worse because it will increase its effort to attract your attention. Many reach this point.

They reach this point, and the lucky ones realise it.

In the Hero's Journey, this first stage is known as the Call To Adventure. This is when the potential hero is presented with a challenge. The word "adventure" is from Latin adventurus meaning "about to happen".

When you can admit that there's something really wrong with how you're living, in how your life is going, when you can make that brave admission, that it is unmanageable, then you are already inviting help in.

So something's about to happen... If you follow the Steps and know the Hero's Journey stages, it's always going to be something supreme that will transform your life.

2. Be courageous enough to ask for help

Step 2: Came to believe that a Power greater than ourselves could restore us to sanity.

What is a Power greater than yourself all about then? It's as simple as this: ask yourself if you are the greatest power in the universe? Certainly – unless you are an extreme narcissist and deluded beyond belief – you will acknowledge that you certainly are not. So then this is a beginning, and this Step can be directed to whatever it is that is a greater Power, whatever you think that might be – or even if you cannot begin to imagine, just the acknowledgement and acceptance of this is fine for now.

Think of a metaphysical and ubiquitous power, an energy. I have known people at this stage have as their greater power, something that is greater than them alone – the Force from Star Wars; the managerial set-up of their favourite football team; nature; the universe; the 12 Steps programme itself; and quite frequently the other people at their 12 Steps meeting ("God" standing here for "Group of drunks/drug addicts"; in recovery it's also been said to stand for "Good orderly direction", "Grow or die", "Gift of desperation" and the "Great outdoors"). One thing to remember though, your Higher Power is not your parent, partner or sponsor!

Then, there is that part of the sentence in Step 2 that says "restore us to sanity". So can you admit that your life and the way you've been living amounts to insanity? The word "sane" derives from Latin sanus meaning "healthy", and "health" is connected with the word "whole", so this can help you look at this. Do you feel healthy and whole? Not just physically healthy, although this is to be included, but emotionally and mentally together? Or do you feel frayed, damaged, in pieces or actually completely broken?

Then there is that use of the word "restore" rather than something like "gain" or "get": so it means that you are starting a process, taking the first steps on a journey, to bring back or re-establish something that you once had. Consider, that no one is born in pieces or completely broken as we are talking about here. It means that something happened to cause the damage to us, to crack us into pieces, to utterly break us. So this is about putting all that back together to make it whole, to make it complete and healthy, to be how you were born to be. And then some more.

In the Hero's Journey stories we have seen the potential hero in their drab normal world, in which they are often such as the child bullied at home and/or school; the partner abused in some way at home; the man or woman bossed about at work and who can never seem to say no or stand up for themselves in any way at all...

When you are fearful like this and are not trusting in life, you will settle for much less than life has intended for you. All seems hopeless. You have been injured and are being played with by your dragon.

But then some information is put in front of this person, some call delivered in some way for them to go into the unknown. It is exclusively for them. They either instinctively know this or are emphatically told it. No one else can go in their place.

But they could still say no, and stay in the familiar discomfort. They may think: "At least the devil I know is better than the devil I don't know..." People, perhaps understandably, will be fearful of taking this risk to try something new and unknown.

But they should be more frightened of staying where they are if it is shattering them, if they feel already dead inside. Time is slipping away. If they already feel broken, imagine how much more shattered, helpless and useless they will be in, say, another year.

In 12-Step recovery terms this person is described as being at "the turning point". It is sometimes put by those who choose the right way to turn: "I came. I came to. I came to believe." This is when the initial decision is pondered: do I go back to the narrowness of that which I at least know – even if it is killing me... or do I take a step forwards into the vast unknown?

Christianity's symbol, so that of the world's largest religion so far in the history of humankind, is a cross, which could be viewed in one way as representing a turning point, a choice, a decision to be made – in a similar way that crossroads are depicted with such significance as representing a location "between the worlds" or where you can sell your soul to the devil.

Consider this, during the crucifixion, on one side of Jesus – who represents love, trust, hope, goodness, and who didn't even have to be there, remember – is the man who became known as the Good Thief and on the other side is the man known as the Bad Thief. The Good Thief says: "Jesus has done nothing wrong." He asks that Jesus remembers him when they have died, he asks for mercy. He trusts Jesus. But the Bad Thief taunts Jesus: "You're supposed to be a master, you should save us" and he insults him. He doubts Jesus.

The crucifixion – that is life, for life is painful, life is suffering: no one but ourselves can feel our own loneliness, our pain, our sorrow, our tragedies, our heartaches, our disappointments, our guilts and our shames – represents the choice we have every day. That choice is to be like the Bad Thief full of resentment, hopelessness, anger and fear or to be like the Good Thief and live our lives by love and trust and hope and goodness. We need to acknowledge this, even if identifying as an atheist, for Western civilisation as we know it is based on this particular Hero's Journey story.

Even avowed atheists look in deep wonder to such as a beautiful sunset or the stars in the night sky after a bereavement of a loved one, and in doing so acknowledge that there is more than we know. On gazing out this feeling dwells deep inside, at the core.

In the AA Big Book's chapter entitled We Agnostics it says that "something like half of us thought we were atheists or agnostics". This was written in the 1930s when church-going was much more of something that people did. So AA membership today is likely I think to have even a larger percentage come into its rooms who identify as atheists or agnostics. The 12 Steps works for any of them as well, so long as they bring humility, open-mindedness and the will to work to get better. This is proven over many decades now.

They say there are no atheists in the trenches, and when something horrifically shocking happens such as a child goes missing we see a community crowd into a church to pray. It is more than we will ever know as we have been designed this way. If we truly knew the magnitude we would crumple, an infinite times more than when we wonder where and if those stars and space ends, and if they ever do, what then?

The symbolism and meaning of the crucifixion was put this way by the psychotherapist Wayne Kemp in The Anxiety Conversation (that was co-authored by this author): "Our crucifixion is on the cross of the lives we lead – in the here and now. So that crucifixion within will bring you to a resurrection. Every human being has to be crucified, we are constantly being crucified in our lives, and so then we have to ask for mercy and have trust and if we hand our lives over to the care of our Creator we have our resurrection and we can be restored to life. Or we can face the hell of progressive pain we create for ourselves due to our powerlessness over the forces of life."

We are powerless over the forces of life. Admit it. Know it.

In both the Hero's Journey and the 12 Steps there has to be an acknowledgment that that which is presently known has become a senseless way to continue, that there is an utter insanity about it. That is about being so resentful, feeling so hopeless, angry, fearful, full of shame and guilt, about just about coping or surviving day by day and sometimes not at all; or that the only way to get through our life presently is by working ourselves towards an early grave in a life where we don't see our children, friends and family and barely spend any decent time at home; or not being our real selves due to drinking excessively or taking the tablets. There are many other ways of avoidance and distraction and of numbing ourselves from ourselves.

There has to be the honest admitting of this, and this needs to be followed by a coming to believe: to believe that something more than what is presently being endured can go to a better place, that we can be guided to return to a former condition, a restoration.

It is this part of the Little Gidding poem by TS Eliot – one of a series of four poems he wrote in the 1940s about time, perspective, humanity and salvation with an emphasis on purgation. The title comes from an English village called Little Gidding that in the 17th Century had a small religious community. As within that religious community, Eliot believed that suffering was needed before a new life could begin.
"We shall not cease from exploration
And the end of all our exploring
Will be to arrive where we started
And know the place for the first time.
Through the unknown, remembered gate
When the last of earth left to discover
Is that which was the beginning."

Belief is a powerful force. I always like to remember that -"lief" is connected to the word "love", and "be-" is linked to Greek phuein meaning "bring forth, cause to grow". Then – bring forth and cause love to grow. It's an inside job. The battle is fought, and won with love, inside ourselves.

So a Call To Adventure... and an adventure always contains a challenge of some sort – that's surely what makes it an adventure (as opposed to say a walk to the local shop for a tin of tomato soup, unless you live in a dangerous place). Because of this definition, to many alcoholics and addicts coming into the 12-Step groups it is often put something like this, as a challenge: "Why don't you try something different?" Then it might be added: "If you give it your all with recovery, say, for three months, can be as enthusiastic about the 12 Steps as you were about your drinking or drug-taking... and only after then, if you don't like it, don't see something much more positive about your life, then we'll gladly refund your misery." It's a provocative dare.

Destiny has delivered the summons, issued the dare. It's time to delve into the unknown... But most people never get past this stage. They want to play it safe and stay in the illusion that is certainty. Many people live their entire life in illusion. They become stagnant and unfulfilled. They are obedient cowards.

Naturally, the unknown is scary to some degree. But to walk into it, the fear of the unknown has to reach a point that is not as terrifying as the fear of continuing as it is presently. You realise that if you don't get as prepared as you can and then try to slay the dragon, then the dragon is going to slay you anyway.

If you don't face them, the things that go after you just grow more powerful. That will make then even more terrifying.

A major reason for going on the Hero's Journey, of completing the 12 Steps, is that fear will be removed. It is, for instance, as mentioned in the previously stated "9th step promises": "Our whole attitude and outlook upon life will change. Fear of people and of economic insecurity will leave us." That's not saying that scary people and economic insecurity will necessarily leave us, but that the fear of them will go away. There are many multi-millionaires who are living in financial fear, desperately running every second under the cosh of fear that they might lose it all, that they are likely to lose it all... Some people who look to hold great status in life live in continual fear of others... It's no way to be.

In myths and other Hero's Journey stories, animals can frequently play a symbolic part at this stage, especially as symbolic of uncontrollable human instincts in the would-be hero. For instance, in Dante's Inferno, while he seeks a way out of the dark forest (representing the unexplored parts of his mind and soul), he is pursued by a leopard, a lion, and a wolf that depict unmanageable lust, pride and greed.

So there is a loud summoning and the word "summon" comes from two Latin words meaning to "secretly warn". So it is. The warning has sounded in the addict, in the depressed person, in the potential hero's mind and soul – this cannot go on like this. That is the calling.

Why could this be so terrifying? We could talk here about how people live by their family blueprints and often that is a plan that means we go to fear and anxiety immediately and the first focus is on lack and what could go wrong, and the focal point stays on this, and anything that we focus on gets bigger.

It's like someone living in a ruin knows they need to destroy the ruin before it collapses on them and crushes them to death, perhaps not instantly either but leaving them trapped in agony, a painful and slow death with too much time to think about what they should have done. Even as they die they will be riddled with guilt and remorse.

But they know that ruin, and they realise that if they knock it down, there will be nothing there for a while. There will be a void. That scares them. Yet they know they need to do this to build their new much better home, one that won't collapse around them and kill them under the weight of the rubble that's trapped them. But that point at which there is nothing there where there was once their ruinous home, even if it was a ruin, is frightening.

Then, you can see how belief is requisite. What can you believe in? This is where it is essential to have humility and an open mind. One belief that is paramount to have is that this is the beginning of the end. And so it is: the beginning of the end of the old life, to start the beginning of an emergence into a new one.

Many get blocked by their intellect, they think that thinking their way out of things can always overcome and take control of nature and destiny. But true humility and an open mind knows otherwise.

This solution to the egotistical intellect is put this way in AA's Daily Reflections book: "It is very difficult for me to come to terms with my spiritual illness because of my great pride, disguised by my material successes and my intellectual power. Intelligence is not incompatible with humility, provided I place humility first. To seek prestige and wealth is the ultimate goal for many in the modern world. To be fashionable and to seem better than I really am is a spiritual illness."

Those who continue to be all solely head-and-drive would do well to study this sentiment that is most often attributed to the Roman philosopher born in Andalucia in 4BC called Séneca (and also a version of it to Joseph Campbell): "The Fates lead the willing, and drag the unwilling."

The Fates were three mythological goddesses depicted as weavers of a tapestry on a loom, with the tapestry dictating the destinies of humans. You can be led peacefully or dragged screaming, but either way you're going to end up at the same place.

It is always more advantageous to ask what is my purpose rather than what is my plan – to ask what is good for me rather than what makes me happy, to search for the answer for what would make life better for you and those around you. It has to be better for those around you first and foremost, because anything done selflessly will never achieve the feelings of purpose and contentment that everyone is seeking. And they are seeking it, because we are made this way.

But of course nothing happens like this unless there is willingness, unless there is that first coming to believe. Until that Call To Adventure is answered.

Then, something completely extraordinary will happen.

3. Be decisive, live by love

Step 3: Made a decision to turn our will and our lives over to the care of God as we understood Him.

In the Bhagavad Gita, the god Krishna says to protagonist and potential hero Arjun: "The important thing is to act, the outcome is secondary."

In actual fact, by taking the action, there is already an outcome, at least a progressive and positive internal one. It is said of Step 3 in AA's Twelve Steps And Twelve Traditions that it is "like the opening of a door which to all appearances is still closed and locked. All we need is a key, and the decision to swing the door open. There is only one key, and it is called willingness."

In the Hero's Journey, the potential hero often becomes reluctant at this point. They may even refuse the Call To Adventure. It's scary going into the unknown, it's so scary going towards our deepest fears.

In the 12-Step groups this is often seen as someone finding a reason why they can't go on with such as attending their meetings and working through the 12 Steps. This is often to do with the word "God" in it, which brings down an intellectual armour as well as prejudice. The prejudice comes from how religion is often forcibly taught at school, a church and/or by parents or other elder figures.

In the case of the church – while organised religion offers so much to so many – it has over the years become so frequently entwined with the State, obvious really as the State never misses a chance to control people. Then the God many are told about is a God who will send you to Hell for not paying your taxes and working all your life in a job you hate. Know your place!

So while the essence of religion is all abundantly good, the whiff of power within the institution has sometimes turned to an overpowering stench. The essence of religion is a spiritual awakening, a learning of how to face life on life's turns, a losing of fear, a gaining of fearlessness, which is a big purpose of doing the 12 Steps. Done in the right way, religion has been and is amazing for individuals. But spirit in some church institutions has so often been beaten away by big ego, and that has put off a lot of people.

Thankfully, the idea of God as your own concept of what that is has worked many millions of times in the 12-Step groups, even for people who say they are atheists: as mentioned, it's just about accepting that there's a power greater in the universe. And if there is still a problem with the word God, just use the word "good" instead. Live by good's will, trust in good.

People refuse to carry on here as well because they are not well, and part of the reason they are not well is because they are listening to that voice, that critical unloving voice trying to get at them – the slanderer, the opponent within – as it will for anything that is good for the soul, it will find excuses for you not to do anything that is a boost to your inner growth. Because it wants to stay in control: it wants to be your master, it does its damnedest to demand you to be its slave. It knows that if you start to grow inside that you may start to know who you are, find yourself again, and that you will tell it, that destructive voice and the negative feelings it causes, where to go. The stronger you get, the weaker it gets. Its all-invasive voice will become a pathetic whimper and then give up even trying (although it's always waiting to take you again if you don't keep growing). There is a catch-22 here in that doing the 12 Steps will allow you to know which thoughts are for you and which are against you. It's another incentive to get them completed.

But it is an often fatal fact, that many do resist at this stage of recovery. The fear of the unknown, the fear of fear, is the greatest fear. Similarly, it's why in Hero's Journey stories there is often a refusal here to the Call To Adventure. This could be from lack of self-confidence – a feeling of not being up to what the call involves. In Harry Potter And The Philosopher's Stone, half-giant half-human Hagrid invites Harry Potter when he tells him he's a wizard, but Harry says: "I can't be a wizard, I mean I'm just Harry."

Fear drifts in like a yellow poisonous gas, the person is under attack within and it grows insidiously until the person is dragged this way and that by fear, they are consumed with fear. At first, fear like this whispers, and the person hears it; then it talks, and the person listens; then it shouts, screams, screeches and hollers and the person trembles and cowers. Soon they will become fear itself, a person who is just scared of everything and everyone, including themselves.

"Refusal of the summons converts the adventure into its negative," Campbell explained. "Walled in boredom, hard work, or 'culture', the subject loses the power of significant affirmative action and becomes a victim to be saved. His flowering world becomes a wasteland of dry stones and his life feels meaningless... All he can do is create new problems for himself and await the gradual approach of his disintegration."

Such as when in The Lord Of The Rings, Gandalf tells Frodo he can destroy the all-ruling One Ring by casting it into the fires of Mount Doom, but Frodo says: "I am not made for perilous quests. I wish I had never seen the Ring! Why did it come to me?"

There needs to be a strong driving force to get through this initial refusal. In Star Wars, Luke refuses Obi-Wan Kenobi's Call To Adventure, and returns to his aunt and uncle's house, only to discover the Emperor's stormtroopers have annihilated it. Now, with a strong reason and an invigorated energy, Luke makes a decision to go ahead with the adventure.

Similarly, those in recovery who make a decision here on Step 3 need to have a potent motivation, and for most of those who work this successfully that motivation is the terror of the terror they know that most people call life. They want to do whatever it takes to put distance between that terrifying way of life and a new way that they can see is full of hope instead of hopelessness. They have to or they know they will die anyway... most likely from a slow tortuous death. Even so, it takes great courage.

Sometimes at this point (as well as at any time throughout the adventure) a threshold guardian can appear. They are small but not insignificant challengers and challenges, not the key enemy – but they will most definitely test the potential hero's resolve. They can even break the potential hero. It might be a friend or one or more people that they have to face who doesn't believe in them or their capabilities. In Harry Potter this is Malfoy and Snape. With someone going into 12-Step recovery it could be a friend, a partner or family member who casts severe doubt on their chances of staying away from another drink, drug, bookie, pornographic website, cigarette or damaging relationship. This sort of doubt can prove to be fatal.

Often it will represent the shadow side, that repressed part pushed down to the surface of the unconscious, that which the person has fought from going anywhere near at all costs, but where they need to go to get what they need. It can cause extreme feelings, as confronting this repressed part can be distressing and difficult.

This is often depicted in Hero's Journey stories as a journey into the unknown: infinite dark space, a remote island, a sprawling dark forest, a deep rapid river heading for a colossal cliff-edge waterfall, a towering mountain shrouded in cloud, a vast ocean (either on it, especially when it's stormy; or deep in it, even all the way right down to the bottom), a city with a dangerous underbelly, a forbidding cave, the belly of a whale, a desert with no end in sight, a scarped steep valley... It represents the journey from the normal and familiar consciousness into the unexplored regions of the unconscious, into that ominous shadow side.

The aim of the adventure is to come out the other side and to be able to then live this way: "Even though I walk through the valley of the shadow of death, I will fear no evil."

The person called to the adventure will be encouraged by seeing someone else who has been where they are now, someone assured and full of vitality, a joyful sparkle in their eyes. That certain someone can guide the new adventurer in the same way that they themselves were once guided.

In the 12-Step groups, one of these people will likely become their sponsor: a more experienced person in recovery, someone further along the spiritual journey as a result of having done the 12 Steps and who continues to live them one day at a time, and that nearly always includes having their own sponsor. It's a progressive paying it forward of wisdom and love.

As described earlier, this is precisely how the 12-Step groups started: when Dr Bob and Bill W started helping each other to stop and stay stopped from drinking alcoholically. They sought out other alcoholics in such as hospitals, many of whom would die. For some months all those they tried to help drank again. It seemed hopeless until they realised that they hadn't been drinking. Finally, they spoke with Bill D, who was strapped down in a hospital bed for the safety of the medical staff looking after him. A week later Bill D walked out of that hospital, a free man, never to drink again. He became the third member of what developed into AA. From there, from those three former drunks who each had an extraordinary transformation, it spread around the world to help transform millions more people, most of who had previously been without hope, many suicidal.

In the Hero's Journey the equivalent of a sponsor is a mentor. Frequently they are an older person – and this is made clear by their (often long) grey hair and/or wizard-esque white beards. They are someone who has trodden a similar path, been on a comparable adventure, to the one the potential hero is being called to go on. As a result of this journey the mentor has been on, they have gained something extraordinary. This is clearly visible.

The mentor can come in at the story's beginning to help with crossing the threshold, but can also come in at other times throughout the story, either physically or into the potential hero's memories and thoughts. As humans we need wise guides – otherwise how do you know you're not being led astray? A mentor doesn't even necessarily need to be met in a physical sense. But a potential hero needs a mentor – the journey cannot be made alone, because a major part of the journey is about finding humility.

It's the same with a sponsor, and most 12-Step people will choose someone they spot at a meeting, someone who they can sit down with while they chat face to face. What is certain is that someone always needs a sponsor to guide them through the 12 Steps in the same way a mentor is always crucial to the successful Hero's Journey. I once heard a struggling alcoholic justify that it was not necessarily vital to have a sponsor by talking about a man he knew of who had been sober at AA meetings for many years without a sponsor. Yet he then went on to say that this man said he felt like having an alcoholic drink every day. This man was then "white-knuckling" it, and that is no way to live. It is not living, it is surviving. He had not answered his Call To Adventure.

Such as addiction is nothing to do with willpower, and neither is long-term recovery. Willpower is something we use to get over the line. No one can live on willpower comfortably because willpower is not a natural state of being. It's to overreach oneself.

A mentor or sponsor will always appear when needed, at the right time. When the student is ready, the teacher will appear. But the student has to be ready: and they need to be open-minded and have humility.

Then a potential hero (as with any new 12-Step person) must be willing to go to any length. A hero needs to become willing to die for what is worth living for... Everyone has to find what's worth living for or we die a death of some sort.

"For those who have not refused the call, the first encounter of the hero journey is with a protective figure (often a little old crone or old man) who provides the adventurer with amulets against the dragon forces he is about to pass," Campbell said. "What such a figure represents is the benign, protecting power of destiny. ... One has only to know and trust, and the ageless guardians will appear. Having responded to his own call, and continuing to follow courageously as the consequences unfold, the hero finds all the forces of the unconscious at his side. Mother Nature herself supports the mighty task. And in so far as the hero's act coincides with that for which his society is ready, he seems to ride on the great rhythm of the historical process."

As Campbell mentions here, frequently the mentor in the Hero's Journey gives the potential hero a gift that will help them as they take their initial steps into that new extraordinary world. It is something that will prove to be useful as well as something reassuring to hold, a reminder of the connection with the mentor and so with the protecting power of destiny. There is the lightsaber that Obi-Wan Kenobi gives to Luke in Star Wars; the gadgets that M (subconsciously for Mentor?) presents to James Bond; and the book that bookshop owner Carl Conrad Coreander leaves for the boy Bastian Balthazar Bux in The Neverending Story.

From 12 Steps group meetings, newcomers usually leave their first – or at least early – meetings with something such as the Big Book or Twelve Steps And Twelve Traditions, a phone number to call at any time of the day or night, a Just For Today card.

In fact, anyone interested in the 12 Steps and the Hero's Journey needs to and would greatly benefit from reading these two astounding AA books; actually anyone would greatly benefit for they're not just for alcoholics: they are so much about life. As well, writing a gratitude list as described in this book's Introduction, and reading and living the Just For Today card because it's a wonderful way to live and if what it says is carried out every day as best you can, it will undoubtedly help you and the world around you.

Just for today I will try to live through this day only, and not tackle all my problems at once. I can do something for twelve hours that would appal me if I felt I had to keep it up for a lifetime.

Just for today I will be happy. Most folks are as happy as they make up their minds to be.

Just for today I will adjust myself to what is, and not try to adjust everything to my own desires. I will take my "luck" as it comes, and fit myself to it.

Just for today I will try to strengthen my mind. I will study. I will learn something useful. I will not be a mental loafer. I will read something that requires effort, thought and concentration.

Just for today I will exercise my soul in three ways: I will do somebody a good turn, and not get found out; if anyone knows of it, it will not count. I will do at least two things I don't want to do – just for exercise. I will not show anyone that my feelings are hurt; they may be hurt, but today I will not show it.

Just for today I will be agreeable. I will look as well as I can, dress becomingly, keep my voice low, be courteous, criticise not one bit. I won't find fault with anything, nor try to improve or regulate anybody but myself.

Just for today I will have a programme. I may not follow it exactly, but I will have it. I will save myself from two pests: hurry and indecision.

Just for today I will have a quiet half hour all by myself and relax. During this half hour, sometime, I will try to get a better perspective of my life.

Just for today I will be unafraid. Especially I will not be afraid to notice what is beautiful and to believe that as I give to the world, so the world will give to me.

They may also leave with a printed copy of the Serenity Prayer: God, grant me the serenity to accept the things I cannot change, courage to change the things I can, and wisdom to know the difference.

This prayer caused great enthusiasm as it struck a chord when AA members first became aware of it in the 1940s, and today it is often said aloud by the group at the end of many AA meetings. It is also inscribed on many of the celebratory coins that are awarded at meetings to people in recognition of specified lengths of sobriety. Other popular slogans on these coins are "To thine own self be true" and "One day at a time".

Although the Serenity Prayer is attributed to American theologian Reinhold Niebuhr from the 1930s, there are much earlier verses with similar

sentiments, such as this written by Indian Buddhist monk Shantideva in the 8th Century:
"If there's a remedy when trouble strikes,
What reason is there for dejection?
And if there is no help for it,
What use is there in being glum?"

As with all great teachers the mentor or sponsor will allow the person to realise what is already there inside them: they are merely the guides to find the vitality, the light, the love, the greater power, the extraordinary force, the divine spirit, the Godness that's already within them. To find the hero inside.

Something here is astounding. The word "heroin" derives from Latin heros meaning "hero" because of its influence on the user. Heroin users say the drug makes them feel intensely calm, in a state of pure bliss. Just imagine feeling like that without having to damage the body and do it artificially… (you can do it). It's also a marked connection that some users smoke heroin by heating the drug on aluminium foil above a flame and then inhaling the smoke through a tube, straw or rolled-up cash note, a method known as "chasing the dragon". So, potential heroes after dragons…

Then the word "alcohol" is from the Arabic term al kuhl meaning "the finer thing" or "the essence": the intrinsic nature or indispensable quality of something. It was specifically used to denote a very fine powder of black kohl that was used by Arab women in the medieval era as an eye make-up to enhance the sparkle in their eyes. The search was for the most pure, perfect form of kohl, that which would give the greatest sparkle in their eyes...

Turn over in your mind another one if you will: the word "spirit" derives from Latin spiritus meaning "breath". A Hebrew word used for "spirit" is ruakh meaning something akin to energy and that includes such as wind and our breath, as well as God's energy that causes plants and trees and us and everything good and of life to grow. It is this spirit that those who are spiritually awoken sense and get to know. It is as such the Holy Spirit in Christianity: God as spiritually active in the world. Alcoholic spirits came to be known as spirits from the fact that the vapour given off and collected during an alchemical process as in the distillation of alcohol was known as a spirit of the original material.

Consider within all this, in the previously mentioned letter that Carl Jung wrote to AA co-founder Bill W in 1961 that he thought a "craving for alcohol" was a low-level thirst for God (verbatim: "the equivalent, on a low level, of the spiritual thirst of our being for wholeness, expressed in medieval language: the union with God."). Jung's letter went on to say "Alcohol in Latin is 'spiritus' and you use the same word for the highest religious experience as well as the most depraving poison. The helpful formula therefore is: spiritus contra spiritum." So "spirit against spirit" – a spiritual experience to counter addiction to the alcoholic spirits. In the letter Jung also put an asterisk after the sentence concerning the "union with God" and at the letter's end he revealed the asterisk, quoting the Bible's Psalm 42:1 – "As the hart panteth after the water brooks, so panteth my soul after thee, O God." A hart or deer is symbolic, standing for honesty, love, kindness, mercy, grace and forgiveness. (Think of the Hero's Journey story that is Bambi produced by Walt Disney, who himself went through a Hero's Journey story as do many creative people and entrepreneurs.) The writer of this psalm speaks of all the desolation he has endured and prays to be saved from loss and ruin. He grieves for his remoteness from God and asks for the renewal of that relationship. What he writes about sounds like depression and anxiety as he says: "My tears have been my food day and night" and how he used to feel protected and happy, but now pleads: "Why, my soul, are you downcast? Why so disturbed within me?"

Furthermore, connected to all of this is the word "elixir", a magical potion or medicinal cure; a substance capable of changing base metals into gold; something that can prolong life indefinitely; a cure-all; the essential principle. The word was introduced in late Middle English, through Latin from Arabic al-liksir that is the Arabisation of Greek xerion, which was used to describe a "powder for drying wounds". This takes on more significance when you realise that the word "trauma", that such as doctor and addiction expert Gabor Maté says is behind every addict he ever saw in his long career, derives from Greek words tetrainein meaning "to pierce" and titroskein meaning "to wound".

Then there is "alchemy", from where the English word "chemistry" derives, from the Arabic word al-kimiya, that is made up from al meaning "the" and kimiya that is from Greek khemia, meaning "art of transmuting metals". It was the medieval forerunner of chemistry, concerned with the transmutation of matter, in particular with attempts to convert base metals into gold or find a universal elixir. So taking something ordinary and turning it into something extraordinary, often in a way that cannot be fully understood. Connected is the "philosophers' stone", a legendary alchemical substance capable of turning base metals into gold or silver, first mentioned in writing in 300 AD.

A beautiful story here. Art experts were restoring the Sistine Chapel frescoes created in the 16th Century by Michelangelo. Adored by people around the world, the restorers soon realised a difficult problem when they saw, to their initial disbelief, that underneath the art that everyone knew so well were brighter colours and more intricate details that had not been seen for centuries.

Then their epic dilemma was: did they restore it to what everyone always knew so well, or did they reveal the brighter version that was actually there all along?

Of course, it's a fantastic analogy for us. Most of humankind has no idea of what is the true magnitude of the bright intricate powerful magnificence within each and every one of us.

There's even more to all of this… The triangle within a circle symbol was adopted as an official AA symbol at an International AA Convention in St Louis in 1955. To this day it is widely used, including many in recovery who wear it as jewellery or have it tattooed. Bill W said about the adoption of the symbol: "The circle stands for the whole world of AA, and the triangle stands for AA's Three Legacies of Recovery, Unity and Service. Within our wonderful new world, we have found freedom from our fatal obsession. That we have chosen this particular symbol is perhaps no accident. The priests and seers of antiquity regarded the circle enclosing the triangle as a means of warding off the spirits of evil, and AA's circle and triangle of Recovery, Unity and Service has certainly meant all of that to us and much more."

Since at least the 17th Century an almost identical symbol was used, except that within the triangle was a square and within the square was a smaller circle. The Squared Circle, as it is known, is an old alchemical symbol created to illustrate the interplay of the four elements of earth, water, air and fire – to symbolise the philosophers' stone.

In 1997 Harry Potter And The Philosopher's Stone by JK Rowling was published. It was the first novel in the Harry Potter series, that are now the bestselling book series in history. This fantasy novel introduced Harry Potter, a young wizard who discovers his magical heritage on his 11th birthday. In the seventh book of the series, Harry Potter And The Deathly Hallows, a symbol for the Deathly Hallows appears: a triangle with a struck-through circle in it. The triangle shape represents the Cloak of Invisibility, the circle depicts the Resurrection Stone and the straight line down represents the Elder Wand. It's all so connected and symbolic, especially here the Resurrection Stone that allowed the holder to bring the dead back to life.

The original resurrection stones were stones of immense weight used to prevent newly buried corpses from being stolen. But there is no resurrection without crucifixion... This is the story in the Bible: that is really a brilliant bookshop in one book. It is a collection of immense stories – 66 books by different authors put together, with the first stories written down approximately 3,500 years ago and taking around 1,500 years to complete. Astoundingly, put together as they are, they have a plot. These stories and this plot are to explain the human condition and this world and how to survive it and thrive in it as a person. Many of the stories are much older than 3,500 years and until written in the Bible had been verbally passed on through the generations. It is no wonder that Western civilisation is based on the Bible's meaning because it reveals a manner of living that, deep-down, we already know as the way we need to live together harmoniously. People try to live other ways... and look what we get.

This is what recovery is, the chance to rise from out of the chaos, to have a new life that's, for the most part, in order. The Hero's Journey.

You are what you are, but you're also what you could be. The person that you're meant to be.

It's someone beautiful and strong who is here for an amazing purpose. Why else would you be here? But you are the only one who can discover who you were born to be.

Many complete Step 3 (although a good sponsor will remind a sponsee of what it means at various apt times during their recovery) by saying, on their knees with their sponsor at their side saying it too, the Third Step Prayer: "God, I offer myself to Thee – To build with me and to do with me as Thou wilt. Relieve me of the bondage of self, that I may better do Thy will. Take away my difficulties, that victory over them may bear witness to those I would help of Thy Power, Thy Love, and Thy Way of Life."

It signifies there's a new set-up in your life. Now you have to keep going, and find even more courage.

As the author Colin Butts put it: "Answer the questions that scare the shit out of you and never give up."

4. Look inside fearlessly

Step 4: Made a searching and fearless moral inventory of ourselves.

So the mentor has shown by the living proof that is their wisdom, knowledge, insight and that often indefinable attraction they have, just exactly what is possible and where to start looking for it. Then it's time for the protagonist of this Hero's Journey to really spring into action. The potential hero has to do something other than looking and listening now. Now is the time to stop talking the talk.

With Step 4 you need to write a list detailing all your life, listing every single one of your resentments and secrets. Everything has to be prepared in order to be put on the table. No if or buts. Every single thing. Including the sort of secrets you wouldn't want your mum to know...! Many of these are things of a sexual nature, for obvious reasons.

It's written in the Alcoholics Anonymous chapter How It Works that: "Half measures avail us nothing." Note that it says "nothing" not "50 per cent". In the same way, 99.9 per cent will avail not 99.9 per cent, perhaps it will be beneficial – but that missing 0.1 per cent is the key. It's possibly the main thing that needs to be put on the table. You won't entirely know what that thing is or things are, so everything has to go down: 100 per cent. Everything has to be admitted, a total clearing out of clutter and more crap. With it will go shames and guilts, remorse and regrets. In its place then can come positive and loving things, emotions and feeling and thoughts that are wonderfully beneficial to you and those around you.

Note too how this chapter title says: How It Works, and not How It Could Work or How It Might Work, or How It Worked For Some People... The 12 Steps are a spiritual sum that will always add up the same, giving the result – so long as they are undertaken thoroughly and honestly. And that means fearlessly.

If there's a cave, or part of a cave, that someone is afraid to go into, then they have not been totally fearless and so they will not gain fearlessness. Fear will still have a hold. As Joseph Campbell said: "The cave you fear to enter holds the treasure you seek."

Such life-saving life-giving priceless treasure is never going to be at the cave's entrance. Or even halfway in. So this is why you have to go all the way in, why you have to explore every single aspect of your life and your reactions and your part in those behaviours. Especially the darkest parts, in the insides of the shadows.

From the AA book Daily Reflections it says: "I must walk into darkness to find the light and walk into fear to find peace. By revealing my secrets – and thereby ridding myself of guilt – I can actually change my thinking; by altering my thinking, I can change myself."

On changing thinking, it's why some people within AA say an alternative meaning for the fellowship's acronym could be Altered Attitudes. It's no use just putting the bottle down: the manner of thinking has to change too, the methods of responding to life on life's terms, the focussing on negativity and lack (such as the humorous but true: "If I won a million on the lottery I'd be fed up because it was two million the week before!").

It's along these lines that AA people say that with alcoholism the alcohol is in the bottle but the "ism" is "InSide Me". It can also stand for "I Sponsor Myself", "I Sabotage Myself" or "I, Self, Me". The first and latter two can apply to everyone. So can the sponsoring oneself if no help is sought and that person in trouble tries to sort everything out alone, that is they attempt to fix their problems with what has quite likely caused at least some of their problems… That just makes for more problems.

Step 4 is about how our human instincts can exceed their proper function, it's to discover our liabilities and to see how guilt, grandiosity or blaming others has a consequence. It identifies negative thoughts, emotions and actions that have ruled life. It reveals how even from the start, by simply having the willingness to look at and list our liabilities, that will bring light into any darkness.

As it is so inspirationally described at the start of the Step 4 chapter in Twelve Steps And Twelve Traditions: "Creation gave us instincts for a purpose. Without them we wouldn't be complete human beings. If men and women didn't exert themselves to be secure in their persons, made no effort to harvest food or construct shelter, there would be no survival. If they didn't reproduce, the earth wouldn't be populated. If there were no social instinct, if men cared nothing for the society of one another, there would be no society. So these desires – for the sex relation, for material and emotional security, and for companionship – are perfectly necessary and right, and surely God-given.

"Yet these instincts, so necessary for our existence, often far exceed their proper functions. Powerfully, blindly, many times subtly, they drive us, dominate us, and insist upon ruling our lives. Our desires for sex, for material and emotional security, and for an important place in society often tyrannize us. When thus out of joint, man's natural desires cause him great trouble, practically all the trouble there is."

It goes on to say that with Step 4 we seek to "find out exactly how, when, and where our natural desires have warped us". This Step will enable you to find a real ability to cope with life and to meet life's responsibilities with your own resources – that are much greater and capable than you might think – and that perhaps it is the case that there's the need rather than to change certain conditions... more so the need to change yourself to meet these conditions. It talks about how this Step is to help anyone doing it to discover "a chink in the walls their ego has built, through which the light of reason can shine".

Step 4 is the discovery and uncovering of what the 12 Steps literature describes as "personality defects", "an index of maladjustments", "major human failings", "serious violations of moral principles" or "defects of character". They are something that everyone has in varying degrees as they are part of the human condition. They are known elsewhere as "sins".

What the hell have sins got to do with this? Hell has everything to do with it, hell on Earth as an entity, a state of being. The word "sin" as originally used was a Greek word for "missing the mark" and it was generally used initially in spear throwing. So what that means is that when you sin, you are not doing the best you can, being the best you possibly can be, not fulfilling the full potential, not reaching the best ideal: you are not there to help others as much as you could, you are causing discontent inside, putting a sort of bad influence or poison into your being.

Why the need to write secrets down on paper to let them out? Because secrets make you sick: a secret is a guilty verdict that the harsh court in your head has given you. Guilty verdicts always come with a sentence and a punishment, and that may be a life term of self-pity, low self-esteem and self-loathing.

Solitary confinement with self is a life sentence that has to be avoided. Many held like this seek a way out through suicide. Yet no one has any idea what it's like if they go this way: it may be to a far worse place, so it's always better to deal with what there is to deal with on Earth, and there is always a solution.

Our ancestors knew all about this. Consider the word "sullen", from Latin solus meaning "alone". Then that the word "hell" is from an Indo-European root meaning "to cover or hide". Secrets make and keep us sick, they keep us in torment, in hell. The word "secret" itself is connected to the word "secede", meaning "to withdraw from membership of an alliance" (to the human race?) that comes from Latin secedere meaning "go away, withdraw, separate", from se- "apart" and cedere "to go". And the etymology of the word "secede" is connected to the word "suicide"...

As too is the word "self" from Latin suus meaning "one's own". Latin sui means "of oneself" then adding -cidium meaning "a killing" and you have the etymology of the word "suicide". The meaning "person who kills themselves deliberately" is from the 1720s. But in Anglo-Latin, the form of Latin used in medieval England, the term for someone who died by suicide was felo-de-se, meaning "one guilty concerning himself" or "felon of self" and "felon" comes from Old French, literally "wicked", connected to fel meaning "evil". This is associated with the word "fall" that is from Old English fallan, feallan, related to Dutch vallen and German fallen;

and from Old Norse fall meaning "downfall, sin". The downfall of self...

Incurvatus in se, Latin for "turned inward on oneself", is a phrase describing a life lived "inward" on and for oneself rather than "outward" for others and God. The sickness of self-centredness and selfishness is bound to lead to a dis-ease: it goes against how we are made to be. Think about it, as if we were made not to care for others, a long time ago humankind would have ceased to exist. It is thought this phrase was first said by Saint Augustine, a philosopher born in 354 AD whose writings influenced the development of Western philosophy. It is about how sin is to be turned inward on oneself and how if a life is lived like this it only gets narrower, colder and darker. It is about the sort of people who have become so turned inward that on seeing other people's happiness they feel pain rather than pleasure.

It is a way of being that frequently ends in suicide. That leaves all those left behind wondering every day for the rest of their lives what more they could have done, which is why it has been said that a suicide often takes more than one life. If you think about all the seven deadly sins they are all about, to differing degrees, being turned in on oneself. It is a deadly way to attempt to live.

In early English common law, an adult who killed themselves was literally then a felon: a person who committed a felony. (This is why frequently people still say "commit suicide", implying someone has committed a crime.) The felony of felo-de-se meant the deceased was given a shameful burial – often with a stake through the heart and with a burial at night with no mourners and at a crossroad: burial at crossroads at that time was the method of disposing of executed criminals and one explanation for these crossroad burials for those deemed criminals is that ancient Germanic groups often built altars at crossroads, and as human sacrifices, especially of criminals, formed part of their ritual, some of these spots came to be regarded as execution grounds. Superstition also played a part in the selection of crossroads in the burial of people who'd died by suicide as some people believed those who died this way could rise as the undead, and so burying them at crossroads would inhibit their ability to find their way if they returned in search for someone to avenge.

Then, why the need to put resentments down as well and let all of these out? Because we must expel these tormenting ghosts. Consider that the word "resent" is from Latin re- "expressing intensive force" and sentir meaning "feel". The early sense was "experience an emotion or sensation", later "feel deeply", giving rise to "feel aggrieved by". So a resentment is when you re-feel something bad, and it means that you are re-living it and feeling once again the feelings of such as anger, hatred and fear. It is known that all addicts are experts at resentments and it's one reason for the habit they have: because those bad feelings keep on coming, often growing in intensity, as the memory will most likely close in on the worst part and repeatedly replay it in slow-motion, much like a sporting slow-motion replay does as it analyses such as a foul. There is a joke that goes: did you hear about the addict who died? They buried him, and then a year later they buried his resentments...

In The Anxiety Conversation, the interview between this author and psychotherapist Wayne Kemp (with a combined continuous 12-Step recovery time of more than 50 years), on this it said: "David: Viktor Frankl wrote fantastically about choice in Man's Search For Meaning about being in a Nazi concentration camp – 'Does man have no choice of action in the face of such circumstances?' He wrote that we do always have a choice, wherever we are in life. 'Everything can be taken from a man but one thing: the last of the human freedoms – to choose one's attitude in any given set of circumstances, to choose one's own way... Fundamentally, therefore, any man can, even under such circumstances, decide what shall become of him – mentally and spiritually... It is this spiritual freedom – which cannot be taken away – that makes life meaningful and purposeful.'

Wayne: Yes, people always have choices. It's the attitude. Are we able to stay in an emotional balance under all circumstances? I am in awe of Frankl, the horrors he went through and yet he managed to maintain that attitude. He's proof of the idea that it's not what happens to us so much, it's how we handle it and how we deal with it, and he chose not to hate. Because he knew it would destroy him.

David: So forgiveness is massive? I heard someone say the clue is in the word 'forgive' as it means to give ourselves something...

Wayne: Frankl was choosing not to hate. We are destroying ourselves if we do.

David: Like drinking poison but waiting for the person we hate to die from it?

Wayne: Exactly. That's why you're advised to forgive people because it only destroys you. I knew a guy whose daughter was murdered and it was horrific for him of course, and he tried to get into the prison to kill this man who'd killed his daughter and he was consumed with hatred for him and thoughts of revenge – then one day somebody said to him: 'That man who killed your daughter is now killing you, he is now destroying you.'"

Incidentally, the word "remorse" is similar: it derives from Latin re- meaning "expressing intensive force" plus mordere "to bite". So when we have remorse it is as if we keep gnawing away at ourselves, from the inside out. No wonder we are less than we should be. It's okay to feel sorry for something and learn from that in vowing to deal with any similar situation differently – but it's not okay to let it eat us up. If it does that we are never able to fulfil our potential, to help others and be our best ideal.

So in Step 4 it is suggested you write down all your secrets and every one of your resentments, in preparation for reading them aloud to another person – remembering that when you asked someone to sponsor you they likely made sure you were "prepared to go to any length". Now excessive pride can rush forward here dragging along self-justification telling you that you don't really need to go this far, and a rush of the soul sickness that is fear tells you not to look this much, if at all as the wounds are too contaminated and infected to even consider an examination.

At this point, you need to look at your sponsor and listen to others who have taken this fourth step and followed it swiftly with the fifth step to hear and see the evidence, the living proof, that if you shove away pride and fear to allow willingness and a commitment to thoroughness and truth to come in instead, then a feeling of a new confidence usually arises. There is as well a great sense of relief at finally facing ourselves. After all, wounds and scars have to be looked at if they are ever to be cleaned up and treated so they can heal. Otherwise the sticking plasters and bandages and stitching up will be on the wrong places, which is what has been happening with the addictions, the dysfunctional relationships and the wrong jobs.

Ask in your heart, feel it in your gut: these never deceive us. To heal means to make whole, not to raggedly attempt to hold it all together.

In Dante's Inferno we see the suffering of the damned, the different levels of ruin in Hell caused by such as lust, gluttony and greed. These are the consequences of how a life is lived: we can be put in a level of hell by these "defects of character" and we have fallen past the notice reading: "Abandon all hope, you who enter here."

A searching moral inventory as is Step 4 is the beginning of the journey deep inside, and a way of coming up into the fresh air and light again. You will breathe easier. Many who leave their first 12 Steps meeting report that they had a feeling of hope for the first time in a long time. Certainly this feeling will grow as the 12 Steps are taken one Step at a time. Simply by becoming willing to do and complete them, your sense of hope will grow.

What you most need will be found where you least want to look.

That which you are scared of, loathe fiercely, find intolerable, that which repulses you and that which you do all you possibly can to stay away from, that is where you need to go to discover what you need to know. It's in the King Arthur (Hero's Journey) story when in the search for the Holy Grail, that contained the redemptive substance King Arthur and his knights needed, they were faced with the fact that it was somewhere in a vast dark forest, and what they had to do was each go into that deep forest at the point where it looked the darkest to them…

It is about discovering something you need desperately but have lost, yet you don't know what it is until you actually find it. Then you find it pulsating from within, then you remember and realise what it was all along. That core part of you. At your heart. You need to set it beating again, make it truly alive by your actions, and it's only you that can do that.

For most people who are not ready, it's likely there is not enough pain yet (or they are just enough masking the pain with such as drink or pills or another addiction that hasn't yet stopped "working"). For these people, they are not terrified enough of where they are to be able to summon up the strength to go forward to where they have to go if they want to go forward. A sponsor or mentor can help you realise you need to go all the way down deep inside to investigate and to find the source of your suffering.

There is a way out but it's through hell. The only way up is down first.

Separation leads to Desperation that leads to Repair. The process is: Uncover, Recover, Discover. Some say the order here is "Uncover, Discover, Recover"... but I don't think you can truly discover what there is to find until you have first reached a level of recovery. You have to get well first before taking the major discovery part of the journey. It's for discussion.

For some people it works if they can imagine vividly enough what life is going to be like if they don't take those first courageous steps, and then carry on.

Again a sponsor or mentor can help here. This is everything about courage: the Buddha is quoted to have said: "A man who conquers himself is greater than one who conquers a thousand men in battle."

There is also another reason why this solution remains a journey that takes place along the road less travelled, and M Scott Peck wrote about it so well in his book that for this reason was called The Road Less Traveled (the title itself coming from a 1916 poem called The Road Not Taken by Robert Frost that contains the lines: "Two roads diverged in a wood, and I–, I took the one less traveled by, And that has made all the difference.") In that book – which became a bestseller initially due to the enthusiasm for it of people attending AA meetings – M Scott Peck wrote: "Being about spiritual growth, this book is inevitably about the other side of the same coin: the impediments to spiritual growth. Ultimately there is only the one impediment, and that is laziness. If we overcome laziness, all the other impediments will be overcome. If we do not overcome laziness, none of the others will be hurdled. So this is also a book about laziness."

The psychiatrist went on to write that in his efforts to help his clients grow, he realised that the main thing stopping this obvious benefit was their laziness. He explained that he had a moment when he finally understood what the Adam and Eve story was about: that they had listened to the serpent and yet not even sought God's side of the story before they ate the forbidden fruit from the tree of the knowledge of good and evil, in which "good and evil" implies "everything" – as in the Egyptian expression said to translate as "evil-good" that is used to mean "everything". So the first people (Adam means "man"; Eve means "living") were not trusting God, they were now playing God to judge what was good or evil. But people were not, are not, designed to go this way, although by being given free will – as is the only loving thing to do with any gift, such as life is a gift – there was always, there is always, this choice at making an attempt to live this way... It's like we know the sun keeps us alive, but look at it and you will go blind, get too close to it and you will become ash. So as soon as Adam and Eve took a bite of the apple, they became self-conscious and consequently covered their nakedness. Then they were banished by God from the paradise they had been in. Interestingly, as a slight aside, the Koran mentions the eating of the apple as being a "slip", which is the same word used in the 12-Step groups when someone succumbs to their addiction again.

Peck carried on by stating that the missing step of Adam and Eve in not asking for God's side of the story is what makes the essence of sin. The debate they could have asked for between the serpent and God is "symbolic of the dialogue between good and evil which can and should occur within the minds of human beings. Our failure to conduct – or to conduct fully and wholeheartedly – this internal debate between good and evil is the cause of those evil actions that constitute sin. In debating the wisdom of a proposed course of action, human beings routinely fail to obtain God's side of the issue. They fail to consult or listen to the God within them, the knowledge of rightness which inherently resides within the minds of all mankind."

He explains that people don't do this because we are lazy, because it takes time, effort and energy to hold such internal debates as these. Then he added that if we seriously listen to the "God within us" we would frequently find ourselves being urged to take the more difficult path, so in deciding to listen to the God within us, we then open ourselves to having to make this effort – that very often is not what seems the easier, softer way. And those last three words of that sentence are another popular 12-Step group phrase, that comes from the How It Works chapter in Alcoholics Anonymous: "Our stories disclose in a general way what we used to be like, what happened, and what we are like now. If you have decided that you want what we have and are willing to go to any length to get it – then you are ready to take certain steps.

"At some of these we balked. We thought that we could find an easier, softer way. But we could not. With all earnestness at our command, we beg of you to be fearless and thorough from the very start. Some of us have tried to hold on to our old ideas and the result was nil until we let go absolutely."

It continues to say that we deal with alcohol, that is "cunning, baffling and powerful". As with, as it is, the enemy within our minds. "The Devil hath power, To assume a pleasing shape," wrote Shakespeare in Hamlet. The 12 Steps help you identify the deceptive shapes that come in front of us in life, to stay ahead of this cunning, baffling and powerful deceiver.

Step 4 in the 12 Steps is about writing down in three columns all your resentments and secrets. An A4 book and a pen so that you can write by hand is the most effective way to do this. It's a harsh realisation but a truth that as well as fear the other thing that will stop you doing this is as Peck says: unmitigated laziness. Know this: the word "lazy" is from Middle Low German lasich meaning "feeble"; akin to Middle High German erleswen meaning "to become weak".

Ensure you have somewhere excellent to hide your A4 book, so that you are not inhibited in any way for fear of it being discovered. Remember, every single one of your resentments – that is, people, places and things that you don't like, that have made you angry, that still make you angry, that bother or have bothered you, irk you in some way, that make you furious, murderous even, or that mildly irritate you whenever you think of them. Anything and everything. Likewise, your secrets, all of them, including and especially any that you were planning on never telling anyone, that you were going to carry with you to the grave.

One useful way to do this is to look back at your life in stages of five years, starting with the present.

Remember people in your life at the time, where you worked, where you studied, where you lived, friends you were with then, holidays and any travel you did, life events such as weddings or funerals and so on. Dig deep. This can and probably will be emotional at times, like looking over all your old photographs, but more so because you will be looking at some things you've repressed and buried. Stop for a while if it gets too much. Although, as with all the Steps, it's hugely beneficial to get this done just remember you are not in a race with anyone. It's useful to have a trusted friend to call on if the emotions rise too high, ideally your sponsor or mentor, an experienced and trusted adviser. Yet another reason not to attempt the 12 Steps alone. However, do not use these high emotions that will most likely arise as an excuse to not do it.

You can in addition start Step 10 at this stage. It's the same, except Step 4 is looking back while Step 10 is for present-day resentments and secrets. It is ongoing. In the beginning this all seems like a tough call, much work and loads of writing. It is, but this is how you are forming your solid foundations built on rock rather than sand.

The more you write down here, the quicker you will learn what makes you tick, how you burn up, what causes reactions and all those feelings; and the more you will understand your part in these and so know what you can do about them (as we are powerless over people, places and things, but we can change our reactions and attitudes: see the

Serenity Prayer for more on this.). When you can identify these things in a split-second – such as: "Right there, I can see pride and self-pity are on their way to grab me here and shake me about a bit, cause me to react in a way I'll regret and then feel sorry for myself for hours – but no you don't!" And then they won't because you've spotted them before they got to you.

So discovering a pattern to these "character defects" helps a person to recognise them and then become capable of stopping them getting in the way of being who they're supposed to be. Listing character defects is <u>not</u> to beat yourself up, but to be able to see what they are and have the opportunity to get rid of them. In which case, more positive stuff can find the space to be let in.

Because you will become increasingly more aware of them coming at you, you will increasingly be able to stop them in their tracks. It's like shining a gigantic bright spotlight directly on them, on these creeping darknesses that try to come at us at every opportunity. When you illuminate them, show them up as they stealthily come for you, they don't make it, they don't even reach you – so they don't get you. As soon as light hits darkness, it always instantly goes.

This is then what it means in the 12-Step promises to "comprehend the word serenity and know peace". It's to understand personal responsibility, to be able to stand tall in spite of and despite whatever comes in life.

And what always miraculously and quite beautifully happens when someone puts the effort in with Step 4 and Step 10 is that fairly quickly, normally within a couple of weeks if they've put the effort in, they will realise something like: "That person cutting me up in their car would have usually driven me mad, but I realise it was mostly my pride that was on its way to mercilessly swing me around, and some self-pity, self-centredness, impatience too, arrogance as well as I didn't really know why they were rushing so much, dishonesty there as well as I've driven like that before, plus some envy as they had a better car than mine – and because I realised all this, all in just a split-second, it didn't even cause a reaction in me. I stayed calm, even serene."

So where you might have previously become furious, for a moment maybe even murderous (because we all have that in us), and then lived in that negative feeling, often for hours as you replayed and relived it over and over again, what happened, what you should have done, what you still could do now, instead it's all over and you can get on with your day. Because it didn't create any bad feeling in you, it didn't cause any resentment, that means there's no need to write it down as a Step 10. You were quite able to stay functioning normally, no strength and vitality was stolen from you over this. This allowed you to have that energy for more positive things, such as helping other people, being the best ideal of yourself that there is – it's notable and quite astounding when this happens, and more and more it does. It's a mental, emotional, physical and spiritual transformation.

Of course, some things will happen that need to be written down. Even those who've been doing this for decades will get some things from time to time. That's okay, as from each of these Step 10s you are still learning about your inner workings. Sometimes you may even be able to consider that person who got a rise in you as a spiritual teacher, and almost, or perhaps even, give thanks to them for doing so... It may be the catalyst to realising that you need to up such as your meditation or 12 Steps meetings or sponsoring someone yourself or any other thing you know that's beneficial to your wellbeing.

This way you will reach a point where, although not inviting things into your life that give rise to resentments, you know that something good can come from them as you discover yet more about yourself. That painfully long queue... You will learn some more about how well you are handling such as impatience, pride, self-pity and self-centredness. That loud music from the neighbour's house... how about listening out instead to your pride, self-pity, self-centredness (these three hunt in a huge percentage of resentments and nearly always as a pack), your intolerance and dishonesty (in that you've played music too loud before, so you are being hypocritical here).

A Step 10 done on the spot as soon as possible, such as immediately, is most effective. You may have to be inventive here, as it's not always convenient to get out the notebook and write stuff down, especially in front of the person to whom you have the resentment. You can instead do it on your phone as though writing a message, or at least do a mental Step 10, which will certainly help, and then remember to write it down later as writing things down has been shown to work best. There have been several times when I've excused myself from a room to do a Step 10, sometimes while I stood in the bathroom. Many 12-Step people also know the benefit of prayer here, especially getting down on your knees, and asking for the resentment to be taken away, and praying for the wellbeing of whoever or whatever led to the resentment. This can be repeated if a resentment returns, and sometimes it needs to be done for a few weeks – until one day you realise you no longer wish the person, place or thing any ill will, which is to your advantage.

If you had a prior resentment against your sponsor, it is advisable to leave that off the Step 4 and write it on the Step 10 list – ask your sponsor what they think on this. Most people will get resentments against their sponsor, as they will tell you how it really is, to help you, and that is not in a people-pleasing manner. Even if you know it's said lovingly, it can lead to a resentment. But know that when you're ready to discover and grow, being challenged by someone who knows what they're talking about and is doing it in a loving way, is one of greatest routes to discovery and growth.

You don't need to read out your Step 10s to anyone else: they are so that you can keep learning about what makes you react in certain ways, although you may choose to read some of them out to your sponsor to release them (especially secrets) or for discussion, perhaps particularly if you find a troublesome pattern. You can destroy your Step 10s once you know the resentment or secret has been dealt with effectively: that is, you no longer feel it, are no longer bothered by it. So many times this can be as soon as it's been written down and read by you.

Make sure to keep your Step 4 and (if you decide to keep any) your Step 10 lists separate though. You will need your Step 4 list to help with Step 8, so keep it until after your Step 8 list is written down on paper. Likewise if any of your Step 10s are concerned with you causing harm to anyone in any way (as AA literature states: "anything that causes physical, mental, emotional, or spiritual damage" to someone; to be spoken through with your sponsor) – keep these somewhere safe until after Step 8 is completed. But don't concern yourself with that Step yet. Taking one Step at a time is what's needed to make the next Step.

So your Step 4 moral inventory is written out by making three columns in your A4 book on each page that's used for it.

In the first column is **the person, place or thing** that the resentment or secret is about (and this column can and often will include the word "Myself" for you will most likely discover just how much self-loathing there is that's affecting you).

The middle column is, as succinctly as possible, for writing **the cause** (and if not based on actual fact or is an opinion acknowledging that by writing "I feel/think that..."). Try to stick to just a few words, a very brief sentence that gets to the real point of it. Cut to the chase!

The third column is headed **this affects my...** and here is written what are commonly known as the seven deadly sins but in the 12 Steps I have seen up to 20, although it is these 14 that I have used: pride, self-pity, self-centredness, selfishness, dishonesty, greed, gluttony, impatience, intolerance, lust, sloth, jealousy, envy and arrogance.

This is written in various similar ways and may have such as the word "fear" listed, although the 14 "defects of character" are the way this author did them. Also, looking at fear, all of these 14 character defects have fear behind them, are a form of fear manifesting itself, usually fear of losing something you have or fear of not getting something you want.

As with all of the 12 Steps I would always strongly recommend reading the Twelve Steps And Twelve Traditions and the relevant chapters on each of the

12 Steps that can be found there, as well as in these chapters of the Big Book: approximately, Chapter 3 More About Alcoholism talks about Step 1; Chapter 4 We Agnostics is on Step 2; Chapter 5 How It Works goes on to Step 3 and Step 4; Chapter 6 Into Action is about Step 5 through to Step 11; and Chapter 7 Working With Others is on Step 12.

So to the moral inventory list, here are the "defects of character" that can be used as a guide for you to decide if one has been affected in order to write it in the third column. (In Step 5 your sponsor will listen out carefully to see if there are any you've missed out or if there are any others he or she suggests you add.)

Pride – it heads the list for good reason, and it attacks in two ways. The high haughty end is that which says inside your head or out loud such as: "How dare you say or do that to the great me!"
The reverse low end, that is shame, says: "What would anyone think if they knew I'd done this/said that/had this done or said to me...?" Sometimes this follows up with: "And that I didn't even say or do anything (to defend or stick up for myself..." or to deal in any upstanding way with whatever it was that caused the resentment).
Self-pity – this is the "poor me", and the wallowing in that. Pride and self-pity are often closely related: Pride comes in on the in-breath, and Self-pity is there as the chest deflates and the shoulders sink. It

can be the thought of such as: "Poor me, that actually happened to me, they actually said that to me, it's only me this sort of thing ever happens to, why always me...?" Sometimes it follows up with: "And I didn't even say or do a thing..."

Self-centredness – most times if you have Pride and Self-Pity, then there is Self-centredness too as it means you're thinking about yourself too much, being egocentric, not considering the bigger picture (that you likely have no idea about).

Selfishness – this is not being kind or generous or giving with your time, money or a skill or talent that you have.

Dishonesty – this is not telling the truth, being deceitful, insincere, untrustworthy. But it is also used here in the sense of being hypocritical: that is, judging someone harshly for something you've done that's similar or having a resentment against someone for something you might do similarly or the exact same if you were in their position. You can even go further and say, if you were that person in their position. It is something like "those who live in glass houses should not throw stones" or perhaps as Jesus said: "He that is without sin among you, let him first cast a stone at her."

Greed – having an excessive desire or appetite for material things, wealth or power.

Gluttony – greed or excess in eating, drinking or taking drugs. (The word "gluttony" is from Latin gluttire meaning "to swallow".)

Impatience – restless, not being able to wait; having or showing a tendency to be quickly irritated or provoked.

Intolerance – unwillingness or inability to accept such as opinions, beliefs, preferences, people, dress or behaviour that's different than yours.

Lust – a self-centred sexual desire in which you are only thinking about yourself, your pleasure or "need" for sex (mostly as a distraction, a refuge from pain, or to escape dealing with problems or feelings).

Sloth – laziness or procrastination, reluctance to make an effort.

Jealousy – fear that your partner or romance or something you have will be taken from you by someone else.

Envy – coveting what someone else has, their possessions or qualities, traits, luck or characteristics. "Envy" is from Latin invidere meaning "regard maliciously"...

Arrogance – having or revealing an exaggerated sense of your own importance or abilities or that you know better.

Write your Step 4 list like these examples, with the headings written at the top of every page of the A4 book that you use:

Person/place/thing	The reason	This affects my
Leah at work.	She said: "You're so lazy."	Pride, self-pity, self-centredness, dishonesty, intolerance, sloth, arrogance.

		selfishness.
Myself.	I got angry with Leah.	Pride, self-pity, self-centredness, intolerance, arrogance.
Myself.	I can be lazy.	Pride, self-pity, self-centredness, sloth, selfishness, dishonesty, arrogance.
The council.	It leaves too many potholes.	Pride, self-pity, self-centredness, dishonesty, arrogance.
Man in the shoe shop.	I feel he dislikes me.	Pride, self-pity, self-centredness, dishonesty, intolerance, arrogance.
My ex-wife.	We didn't have sex enough.	Pride, self-pity, self-centredness, impatience, intolerance, lust.
My sister Sam.	She earns more than me.	Pride, self-pity, self-centredness, greed, sloth,

		envy, arrogance.
Dad.	He always says how well Sam does.	Pride, self-pity, self-centredness, dishonesty, intolerance, sloth, arrogance.

There are some in the third column that would be up for discussion if this was read out to a sponsor. This is why it's so much better to read these out when doing Step 5 to someone who's been through them themselves.

Note how it says "I feel" (or it could have been "I think") unless it's a certain fact with the "man in the shoe shop" as perhaps he didn't dislike whoever wrote this Step 4, perhaps he was worried about something and whoever wrote this Step 4 just mistook his look for dislike towards them, and maybe that was actually much more to do with their self-esteem. Much of the resentments you have are, you will discover if thought about this way, quite possibly only in your head.

Mistakes that people frequently make, especially initially until they get to know the character defects and get in the rhythm, are missing out one or more of the defects of character when there are actually two or three more there. Sometimes on the other hand people write down a character defect or more than one that isn't correct.

As well, naming the wrong person/place/thing in a resentment. Or putting down just one reason for a resentment when really it's more than one, and so it needs to be divided like this. Likewise, only writing one person down when in fact it's more than one that is part of the resentment.

You need to learn about these character defects this way because such as excessive pride or too much self-pity, impatience, sloth, lust, envy and so on will always block you from being who you are capable of being, of being your best ideal, and so who you are really supposed to be. They are a hindrance, and in many cases a downright liability. They block out your assets to varying degrees or completely in some cases. They can and frequently do waste or wreck lives.

As previously mentioned, you may also, to your shock and dismay, realise just how much you resent yourself. This is not good. This can be living in a self-imposed hell, and you need to get out of there as quickly as possible.

As anyone "re-feels" what is it that's causing the resentment, each time they are hurting themselves, that drinking of the poison but waiting for the person, place or thing with which they have the resentment to die. Secrets are a self-administered poison too. This putting them down on paper and then reading them out to another person in Step 5 is a way of banishing them.

Sometimes it's extremely uncomfortable looking at these resentments and secrets. But you have to realise that if you can recall them, they are still there inside you – and they are not doing you any good at all. Consequently you could be living a better way and that would benefit you and the world around you.

What if there are criminal offences that are kept secret? Pages 78 and 79 of the Big Book have more on this, but basically it is: "Reminding ourselves that we have decided to go to any lengths to find a spiritual experience, we ask that we be given strength and direction to do the right thing, no matter what the personal consequences may be. We may lose our position or reputation or face jail, but we are willing. We have to be. We must not shrink at anything."

It is why a few pages earlier in the Big Book it says: "Such parts of our story we tell to someone who will understand, yet be unaffected. The rule is we must be hard on ourself, but always considerate of others." It says in the Twelve Steps And Twelve Traditions that as well as a sponsor someone may choose somebody else, examples including a clergyman or your doctor.

Assets should also be noted while doing Step 4. These are your character assets such as patience, tolerance, kindness, loyalty, forgiveness, humility, loving. The character defects will have blocked these good qualities to varying extents. Now new space is being created to allow them back in and to flourish.

So it is not about reliving old wounds for the sake of it, or going over events and things and people that should remain in the past. It's about clearing them out, throwing out damage to make room for the real you who should be there. Then, as well, getting to understand something about the damage to avoid getting in a similar damaged condition all over again. Sickness reaches depths; the depths are the sickness.

But there is a way out, guided by someone who has got out from those depths. It says in Step 4 that you need to be "searching and fearless". You cannot become fearless by thinking you want to be fearless: the characteristic of fearlessness only comes from being fearless.

In the Hero's Journey this part of the story is about getting ever more ready. It's about being as fully prepared as possible to cross the threshold into the great unknown and all that it holds.

If you have reached this place, it's like David Bowie said: "I don't know where I'm going from here, but I promise it won't be boring."

5. Tell someone you trust with all your heart every one of your heartfelt secrets

Step 5: Admitted to God, to ourselves, and to another human being the exact nature of our wrongs.

Yes, you do need to say about that one, that secret too. This stage, this Step, is the leaving of the known limits into a realm of unknown limits.

"The usual person is more than content, he is even proud, to remain within the indicated bounds, and popular belief gives him every reason to fear so much as the first step into the unexplored," explained Joseph Campbell. "The adventure is always and everywhere a passage beyond the veil of the known into the unknown; the powers that watch at the boundary are dangerous; to deal with them is risky; yet for anyone with competence and courage the danger fades."

In recovery terms it is the turning point decision on which way to go in life. For the alcoholic it is standing at the pub door but rather than opening it, turning around and walking the other way. It is when their hand that has been placed on the handle of a door into the 12 Steps meeting room actually turns the handle and opens the door. It is the moment in a

12 Steps meeting when they realise that when people say they "walk through the door" or "enter the rooms", as they frequently do say, it has much more significance than just walking in: it is in fact a spiritual statement, a vow of intent. It is saying: I am responsible for my life, and I can do this. Here I am, this is me.

When someone going through the 12 Steps starts to read out their resentments and secrets – all of them, no stone left unturned, everything put down on the table – they are really setting out now to a most extraordinary place. The result if done thoroughly and honestly is totally transformational: this is a spiritual law that applies to everyone with the human condition.

A change is being put into action. You have to step into fearlessness, you must walk the walk. But there may well be more resistance. Many people doing the 12 Steps stop here. The threshold guardian appears too formidable... fear grasps hold. They go no further at this time... They will go back to the humdrum, the grey and drab, the making do. The addiction, the mental disease, the spiritual sickness, the codependency, the crime, the not living, the dying a slow tortuous death.

But for those that do cross the threshold it is plus ultra – "further beyond" – the Latin phrase that's Spain's national motto, that's a reversal of the original phrase non plus ultra meaning "nothing further beyond". This was said to have been inscribed as a stark warning on the daunting Pillars of Hercules – the rocky towering promontories that flank the Strait of Gibraltar, which marked the edge of the then known world for the Spanish people. The motto was turned around though to encourage Spanish explorers to ignore the old warning, to have no fear and go beyond the Pillars of Hercules, Hercules being a Roman hero of superhuman strength and courage.

It is the knowing that somewhere, deep inside the deep inside, there is the fearlessness and courage to face the darkest cave you as the leading character can ever imagine, with the most forbidding fire-breathing fear-breeding dragon guarding it, and to enter that cave and slay the dragon to reach the treasure it guards, deep inside the deep inside… It's entering the darkest part of the forest that you can see, where there is no trail, and so having to tread your own path. It is the first realisation that it is possible for a person to go beyond the two cherubim on the veil of the Holy of Holies.

The world the hero goes out to confront holds untold infinite promise, but it can also be ominously threatening. So who is it that can possibly do any of this? The answer is: all of us, for the hero is inside everyone. We're made so.

At this stage though the mentor's support is most definitely needed, that encouragement and wise words from someone who has taken a similar journey and gone beyond, from the ordinary world into the extraordinary world, and made it back again to tell the tale. Similarly, recovery cannot be effectively ventured into alone, as it is never on your own terms. You need the guidance, knowledge, wisdom, you need to see and hear the living proof. You need a dragon slayer. You need a living conduit to the power within you, and so to the greater power. You need someone who has themselves stepped from the dark side into the light. Someone who consequently carries the light inside and who can also because of this see all the light you cannot see.

This is someone who has not just theorised or wished or imagined or talked about it endlessly at parties... This is someone who has fearlessly gone to the place they least wanted to go to in order to get that which they most needed. They have gone through the darkness to find the light. It is not someone who has written all the books and got all the initials after their name if they have not been there. You cannot expect that.

Beware of wisdom that has not been earned.

So this is a big life-changing moment, and Step 5 requires all of your resolve, described perfectly well in the Twelve Steps And Twelve Traditions. "All of AA's Twelve Steps ask us to go contrary to our natural desires... they all deflate our egos. When it comes to ego deflation, few Steps are harder to take than Five. But scarcely any Step is more necessary to longtime sobriety and peace of mind than this one."

For anyone who does read out their Step 4 list to another person and God, as they understand God, there will be a feeling of being at one and belonging. Loneliness and that sense of isolation will leave. Dante wrote: "The deepest isolation is to suffer separation from the source of all light and life and warmth."

Humility will grow in the new light, in fact humility increases the warmth of the glow. There will be the initial glimpses of the realisation of who you really are.

You will know the meaning of grace. Many people doing the 12 Steps who said they were agnostic or atheistic say it was during this stage when they first felt the presence of something greater in the world.

Everyone can be a hero, but not everyone – by a long way – becomes a hero. If you do take this route, you will be on the road less travelled, the broad golden way that leads to a purposeful and fulfilling life, that reaches new freedom and happiness. In AA's Big Book it says: "We feel we are on the Broad Highway, walking hand in hand with the Spirit of the Universe." It is an external adventure and an internal journey. Jesus said: "For many are called, but few are chosen." The external call goes to everyone; but only the elect experience the internal call.

Confessing like this to another person is, of course, nothing new: in every century it has been something in the lives of all spiritual people. Some religion today still has confession as a part of it, so too does psychology in which a session with a coach or counsellor most often involves the deep need every human being has for practical insight and knowledge of their own character flaws and for a discussion of them with an understanding trustworthy other person, and that means talking about, admitting and realising the truth.

With Step 5, now you need to read your Step 4 list out to the Universe/a Higher Power/God/Something That Has More Power Than You Alone plus another person. This is where a trusted sponsor or other mentor is essential. This person is there to guide you, as they have done this themselves (certainly this is the best way), but also so that you can realise you are quite human with everything that you read out, and see that another person will still love and care for you after hearing your each and every resentment and secret. To let you know you are not alone in what you've done or what you carry inside as well as to encourage trust, they will likely let you know a few of their very similar secrets and resentments, with different names and places but with the same reasons, drives, flaws, feelings and reactions.

You will realise that you were not so different at all, that you are not on this planet as someone who is so different from others, not now and not throughout the history of humankind: you will know that there were people who lived ten thousand years before with the same reasons, drives, flaws, feelings and reactions. You will never feel lonely or as alienated and isolated again. You will begin to get the feeling that you are being forgiven... because you truly are. You start to sense that you can truly forgive others too.

You need someone trusted here to hear you because it's essential to make sure you're not deceiving yourself, as you may have done in many ways in life, as many of us do – such as by what is known in psychotherapy as "idealisation", whereby you convince yourself that something or someone was better than they actually were or at least not as bad or as evil: this is to avoid the pain of facing the truth, of looking at the wound, of admitting that your soul is crying for you. Then there's such as repression, suppression, depression, and more, all manner of as the words suggest pressing things down.

For most of us, it is the case that we cannot appraise ourselves even-handedly at all. This is because such as self-esteem, self-image, irritations and anger can lead us to cover up some of our character flaws or we convince ourselves that they are without doubt caused by other people. On the other hand, an excess of self-condemnation, pangs of a guilty conscience and deep regret can lead to a magnification of our fallibilities.

If you are to truthfully realise and acknowledge who you really are on the inside, you need outside help, from someone who knows what they're doing – and, again, someone who has been there and done it is always best by far. It's this scenario: you are trapped down a deep dark hole and desperate to be free, when someone appears at the top and tells you that they have written five books about getting out of deep dark holes, have studied it for 20 years and have a degree in it. Then next to them appears someone else who says they have been down that deep dark hole too and they know a way out. They ask you if you'd like them to help you get out. Who do you choose?

Perhaps you know that you have to share with this person some things about yourself that you sense another person ought to know. You would be much better off to speak with someone who is experienced in this. Intelligent as they may be, you wouldn't ask a doctor how to build a house. Here the listening ear you choose is vitally important if you want to hear the right suggestions and advice delivered in the right way come back to your listening ear. Looking at matters of the spirit on your own, especially in early years, is reckless.

As you read out your Step 4 list you will realise what everyone else who has done so before you has realised: that we don't always – or in fact often at all – know the bigger picture about other people and their situation. A little story, but also a great one: a man had been working nights as a carer at a hospice where just a few hours previously one of the elderly women there who he'd become very fond of had died. He had held her hand as she took her last breath. He was exhausted, which is why he fell asleep on the early-morning bus home. When the driver woke him up at the last stop, the man explained he'd gone way past his stop and so the driver said he could jump off at the right place on the return journey that he was about to start off on now – but that for some point of an official company regulation the driver had to ask the man to get off the bus and get back on it at the bus stop that was the start of the journey just around the corner. "No need to pay again, just jump on," said the driver. "Sorry, I know it's a daft rule, but I've got to get going now as I'm already 15 minutes behind schedule."

So the man got off the bus and in the wind and cold lashing rain he dashed round the corner and saw the bus there with its doors open. He ran and jumped straight on but just as he nodded at the driver he heard a barrage of angry insults fly at him. He looked round. There was a long queue that he'd hardly even noticed. "Oi mate!" shouted someone, their face twisted in anger. "Get to the back of this bloody queue! I've been waiting here in this damned cold and rain for ages as well – why do you think you're so bloody special then?!" Several others there followed that up with more direct and offensive one and two-word insults.

We don't always know the big picture. Frequently we don't know anything of it at all. One of the ever-present resentments of this modern world is the driver who cuts someone up as they race by them. Now 99 times out of 100 it's likely it's just someone driving badly and too fast, a self-centred person who threatens everyone. But, firstly, depending on what mood you are in, you will either shrug your shoulders, utter a verbal curse at them, or want to chase them for 100 miles until they stop and you can get out and punch them. Same situation, different reaction, and that's all to do with you. Then there's the big picture aspect: maybe, just maybe, that person is rushing to a hospital because they've received the call they've been dreading for the past few months. Maybe. And wouldn't that completely reverse any state of vexation, any bad feeling, our ill will, any resentment, we have for them. We just don't often know the big picture.

In Hero's Journey stories this stage is the great leap of faith into the unknown: Neo on the ledge high up the building in The Matrix (although he doesn't take it at first and ends up captured); Harry Potter running at the London King's Cross railway station wall on Platform 9¾. There is a danger of death. For many potential heroes, this is the point of the true beginning, and it symbolises the hero's willingness and commitment to take on the quest. It is the revealing that the potential to be a hero is making a significant move forwards.

"Potential" derives from Latin potentia "power", so this stage is showing the power is there: it's a greater power than has been known before taking this step. Who wouldn't want some greater power? God knows, we need it.

It's crossing the threshold. Into the unconscious. The point of no return here. It's the death of the old to allow the birth of the new.

In real life it's akin to leaving home, quitting that job, travel to a new country, seeing life completely differently due to a life-changing event such as the coronavirus pandemic or the bereavement of a loved one. It brings to mind that the greatest regret of the elderly or those dying is nearly always not trying something that required some faith – be it for such as love, a vocation or travel. They never even answered the Call To Adventure let alone go on any part of that adventure. Never is there much regret for trying something that didn't work out or even that completely failed. The greatest regret for those now with not enough time left is always something for which they lacked confidence (from Latin meaning "having full trust"). Incidentally, "vocation" meaning "a strong feeling of suitability for a particular career, occupation or place in life" derives from Latin vocare: "to call". Unless you want to die with your music still inside you, always answer that call.

Now just imagine if you could always have full trust – in yourself and in the world at large: that is just what the 12 Steps are about, that is where the

182

Hero's Journey goes. If you know fearlessness, if you become fearless, then you can do anything.

If you choose this, if you take responsibility, if you stand tall, if you find your true heart, (or even if you still have to fake it to make it just yet) – if you read out loud to another person your Step 4 list, all of it, watch how the rocket blasts off, and Dorothy sets out on the Yellow Brick Road.

This is a commitment. It is when separation moves towards initiation. It is the point of really leaving the ordinary world and entering the extraordinary world. An infinite prize awaits for anyone who goes this way and continues. It is the knowing and believing that base metal can be turned into gold.

And you need to know here that one of the whole points of this is so that one day you return and give away what you have gained in order to keep it. When the rocket returns to Earth, you will need to – and want to – share the light of the stars with everyone you can.

It could even be known as the success of love.

6. Ask believe receive

Step 6: Were entirely ready to have God remove all these defects of character.

At this stage in the Hero's Journey, the potential hero encounters tests, allies and enemies. Or I prayed to God for courage, and God gave me difficulties to overcome that I could become courageous. To become entirely ready. You can see all of these tests, trials and tribulations in many of the Greek myths, biblical stories, bestselling novels and Hollywood classics.

These are tests so you're prepared for the ordeals that are ahead. You have learned what has been blocking you from being the best ideal you can be. Now you need to look to get rid of those liabilities. You are continuing the training in how to slay the dragon, and you need to be the best prepared you possibly can be.

Very often these can come as things that we really don't feel like we want or deserve in our lives. But the spiritually awoken learn how to give thanks for the sort of things that appear to be problems and hindrances. They will give thanks for them and ask what it is that it is meant to be teaching them, what is it showing them, in what general direction are they being guided?

As this process is about becoming spiritually awoken, look to those who are further along this spiritual journey and try to do as they do. So next time something seems to come in your way, be it a person or a some thing, give thanks for it and ask to whatever greater power you can believe in at the moment: what is this for, what is it to teach me, what can I learn about myself, where should I be going in my life?

This Step comes straight after Step 5 with good reason: it is now that the person in recovery will know the full flaw of their instincts that in great part led them to such as drink excessively, take the drugs, gamble into debt or be a stressed-out workaholic alone again. These are the problem characteristics, the "defects of character", that have been holding them back.

They originate from natural God-given characteristics given to us all to help the human race survive and thrive, but they have become excessive, defective, a way of desperately seeking to fill the gaping aching hole in the soul. They have become a burden that cause trouble in every way. They are fear in its various forms. They stop anyone consumed or controlled by them from hitting the mark, of being the person they are supposed to be. They stop your divine destiny.

In the Twelve Steps And Twelve Traditions it says of our natural desires that far exceed their intended purpose: "When they drive us blindly, or we wilfully demand that they supply us with more satisfactions or pleasures than are possible or due us, that is the point at which we depart from the degree of perfection that God wishes for us here on earth. That is the measure of our character defects, or, if you wish, of our sins."

We can ask for them to be taken away, as we are on our knees. Being on our knees is a humble position that acknowledges we are powerless alone over these things. And it works in exactly the same way that we asked to stop drinking or taking drugs or gambling or working too much or any of the other burdensome stuff. We are inviting a greater power in – which could range from the knowing that now you are asking, believing and receiving help from another person that you are stronger for this, to an utter belief in God. Some people in going on their knees this way have reported that they've heard a question in their mind: will you let me take them away from you? The answer has to be: yes!

It's not instant. It takes time, it takes dedication and discipline, it takes believing through adversities, it takes keeping at it with your feet firmly on the ground when you are celebrating major achievements. Maybe consider that you are being tested to see if you're the one up to this. You always are up to it, because we are all made that way – but you have to prove it. You have to earn this privilege.

So now the person on this Hero's Journey knows what has been holding them back, what has been the cause of most if not all of their troubles, they have to become "entirely ready" to let them go, to have them taken away. And that doesn't mean the defects of character such as pride, self-pity, jealousy or impatience have been swiftly and immediately removed, it just means the person has reached the stage where they realise and know that if they want to move forward, to be the person they're supposed to be, to be their best ideal, these have to be gone.

How would a great leader check someone is really ready? With tests. So things are put in front of the story's main character or person in recovery that test if they're up to it, responsible enough, and then to ascertain if they have the responsibility that comes after they slay the dragon. Can they not only slay the dragon, but can they handle themselves afterwards in the power and glory of that?

So, for instance, something that might happen to a person in recovery is they are given a situation that in the past caused a great deal of emotional disturbance. A common example could be that they are cut up in a traffic jam by someone pushing in. Are the character defects of such as intolerance, impatience, self-pity, self-centredness, selfishness and pride (a reminder: both the haughty high end of pride: "how dare they do that to the great me!" and the low end of pride: "what would people think of me if they knew I'd let that happen?") — are they still out of control to create chaos and disorder and so control the person; or are they in order?

Another example is that temptation might be put their way. The word temptation comes from Latin temptare that actually means… "test". This you have in everyday life, whether in recovery or not, and this you have in many of the most popular stories. Think of James Bond, when a beautiful woman comes to tempt him, and she turns out to be an agent for the enemy. So can temptation be resisted? To the addict in recovery it might be that an old "friend" offers them some drugs. For free. They put the drug in their face, right up to their nose. This is the part where they encounter allies and enemies. In this case the old accomplice is the enemy, and the recovering addict might turn to their sponsor or another person in recovery as the ally.

Or they might relapse, and so fail the test that would allow them to move on to the next stage, take the next step, reach the next level. In recovery terms this is the next spiritual level. In 12-Step terms they will need to go back to Step 1, to admit that they are powerless. It seems they have not yet fully realised this, and so rather than taking the next step on the ladder they have slipped down the slippery snake that is temptation. This is necessary because they will not be up for what lies ahead. They need to go back to put some new training in, back to the start, back to basics. It's not the end, and indeed it could well be their beginning.

In Hero's Journey story terms if the test is passed, it might be that they gain sight of entry to the next room, or the new country or the wherever it is they are going to get their treasure, whatever the treasure may be, in James Bond's case saving the world. Or they fully know they are approaching the darkest cave. And they are willing. They have found a greater power inside themselves. It was always there. At each test, trial or temptation, fear has to be overcome.

We must be entirely ready to have all of our defects of character removed from us. If there are any we want to keep hold of, even a little bit, we must discuss this with our sponsor, our mentor. We must find out why. We need to imagine our life without them.

If Step 5 has been done thoroughly and fearlessly it should be clear that all defects of character arise from the need to feel approved of and loved. They are a consequence of some form of a failure of love. They are all to do with that fear. To move forward, to reach the next level, it is necessary to walk through this fear.

AA's Daily Reflections book tells this brief story about the required change that's needed. "During the first three years of sobriety I had a fear of entering an elevator alone. One day I decided I must walk through this fear. I asked for God's help, entered the elevator, and there in the corner was a lady crying. She said that since her husband had died she was deathly afraid of elevators. I forgot my fear and comforted her. This spiritual experience helped me to see how willingness was the key to working the rest of the Twelve Steps to recovery. God helps those who help themselves."

In Hero's Journey stories such as Pinocchio or Jonah in the Bible, the belly of the whale (or an enormous fish) represents the final separation from the hero's known ordinary world and self. Just like the story about the elevator. By entering this stage, the person will have to be prepared to undergo a metamorphosis. The belly represents the womb, and being inside it indicates they are ready to be born once more. It is symbolic of a death and a rebirth.

For example, Jonah refuses God's command to him to preach repentance to the city of Nineveh for its sinful ways of living or the city will get destroyed. But Jonah didn't want to go and see the king he had to visit to do this, and so he plans to run away by sailing to a place called Tarshish (which means "examination"...). However, while on the boat a storm blows up, and the other sailors on board decide Jonah is to blame. He tells them that by refusing God's request he has angered God – and the storm is the result of that refusal. To calm the storm he tells them to throw him overboard. When they do, the storm stops.

Rather than drown, Jonah is swallowed by a giant fish. Over three days inside its huge dark belly,

Jonah commits to God's will. Finally he is vomited out and he reaches the shore. From there he goes to Nineveh and tells its inhabitants that they must stop living sinfully. The city survives.

Then in The Empire Strikes Back, Han Solo and Princess Leia take shelter in a cave that turns out to be a space slug's belly. While there, they begin to exhibit their repressed romantic feelings. It seemed the love had died but it is now rekindled.

"The idea that the passage of the magical threshold is a transit into a sphere of rebirth is symbolised in the worldwide womb image of the belly of the whale," said Joseph Campbell. "The hero, instead of conquering or conciliating the power of the threshold, is swallowed into the unknown and would appear to have died.

"This popular motif gives emphasis to the lesson that the passage of the threshold is a form of self-annihilation. Instead of passing outward, beyond the confines of the visible world, the hero goes inward, to be born again. The disappearance corresponds to the passing of a worshipper into a temple – where he is to be quickened by the recollection of who and what he is, namely dust and ashes unless immortal.

"The temple interior, the belly of the whale, and the heavenly land beyond, above, and below the confines of the world, are one and the same. That is why the approaches and entrances to temples are flanked and defended by colossal gargoyles:

dragons, lions, devil-slayers with drawn swords, resentful dwarfs, winged bulls. The devotee at the moment of entry into a temple undergoes a metamorphosis."

All birth is painful. A woman in labour; or Mother Nature with earthquakes, tornadoes, eruptions, scorching lava, and powerful rivers carving their way through the earth that then creates a brand-new landscape. Or on another scale but as with William Blake's "to see a world in a grain of sand", a seed breaking in the ground. If we didn't know what was about to happen, we would think the seed was finished, broken, dead – but in fact it has to break to allow the growth from within its dark belly of the soil, to then reach its full majestic potential. To become its greatest ideal. In that perfect condition it is then able to be most beneficial to that which is around it too, from the bees that feed on it to the old lady in her garden who feels floaty at its beautiful scent and sight.

Measured in different time frames a bad thing can sometimes be seen to be a good thing. And, we must remember, we humans are so small in the elaborate magnificence of the universe. Sometimes the sweeping away of many of us in such as the coronavirus pandemic, although for us making up so much tragedy, could be seen as the equivalent of us building a lovely home and going out one morning to see an ant's nest threatening it, so we scoop it away with the brush of our foot without a second thought...

Put in psychological terms, breaking down is waking up; reaching rock bottom is the way to the top. Or as the Twelve Steps And Twelve Traditions puts it: "Delay is dangerous, and rebellion may be fatal. This is the exact point at which we abandon limited objectives, and move toward God's will for us."

This stage of the journey is the realisation, it's the realisation to be fully prepared to face up to what may come – and to do everything needed to be entirely ready for that.

7. Always be humble

Step 7: Humbly asked Him to remove our shortcomings.

In recovery, being now wise to your character shortcomings, you must dig even deeper to get rid of that which is still holding you back. You have to do this to make room for that which will allow you to go fearlessly forwards.

As stated, you need to ask for that. It's a continuance of the admittance in Step 1 that you are powerless, and to invite a greater power inside to rediscover the potency that is there.

Then, with some sort of newly discovered strength from within (and the knowing that in fact it has always been there), the hero stands looking at – with a crystal-clear view – the cave where the dragon guards the treasure. Asking to have shortcomings removed here is like asking for the greatest dragon-slayer ever to help you get rid of an old rusty and cracked armour for the latest one that's shiny and new. Otherwise it's as if you are St George but your armour is corroded and flaking away, the joints don't work properly, your visor is dented so you cannot see much, you have a sword of straw and instead of a shield you are carrying a big boulder. Like this, you don't stand any chance of becoming a legendary hero.

It's like the story of the man clutching to his chest a heavy rock who's drowning in the ocean when a ship called Recovery sails close to him. On deck there are hundreds of people shouting at him to drop the rock. They are shouting that they used to carry a similar heavy rock everywhere with them and it nearly pulled them down to the bottom too. The man hears them, but he shouts back: "Drop this rock – never! It might be making me sink, but it's my rock!" The people on the deck watched him disappear underneath to the dark depths, never to be seen again.

This is like the moment in the heart transplant when the surgeon removes the defective heart and puts it to one side before picking up the new heart to slot it in the space that's been made. This is that moment, the point at which there is, for now, no heart in the body. This moment had to happen because the old heart was broken, blocked, hard and cold, and any moment it was going to stop beating. With the new heart in place, the person feels their reborn heartbeat start beating. Then they realise it is actually the heart they had all along, only that it's been cleaned of all the debris that was stopping it pumping with the strength and vitality it was made to from when it took its first beat. They know they have a new chance.

The road of trials is a series of tests that the potential hero must undergo for the total transformation. Often the potential hero fails one or more of these tests. More of the same will be put in front of them. Eventually, if the potential hero is to become a hero, they will overcome these trials that are in the same manner, and then be able to move on to the next step.

Speaking about the main character in the Hero's Journey, Joseph Campbell said: "It may be that he here discovers for the first time that there is a benign power everywhere supporting him in his superhuman passage. The original departure into the land of trials represented only the beginning of the long and really perilous path of initiatory conquests and moments of illumination. Dragons have now to be slain and surprising barriers passed – again, again, and again. Meanwhile there will be a multitude of preliminary victories, unsustainable ecstasies and momentary glimpses of the wonderful land."

It is amor fati – a Latin phrase meaning "love of one's fate" used to describe an attitude in which someone sees everything that happens in life, including suffering and loss, as good or at least necessary for growth. It is the realisation that emotional pain, as with all physical pain, is to attract the person's attention to something, something that needs to be addressed, changed or avoided from now on.

So this is the beginning of a knowing that – often despite what was learned during childhood – the world is a loving world rather than a hostile world, and that emotional pain is always a signpost pointing to a direction where you become the person you're supposed to be. The sign may read: "To where your inside matches your outside."

That person you're supposed to be is never someone, for instance, riddled and debilitated by anxiety or depression, conditions that always stop someone fulfilling their full responsibility and, that means, their complete and perfect potential in this world.

The need to have shortcomings in character removed is ever there as the potential hero faces more of those temptations, trials and tests – that may lead him to abandon or stray from his goal. That's what the story of Odysseus is about in the Greek epic poem attributed to Homer when on his return from Troy he sails past the Sirens, and the Sirens are the women on the rocks who sing their song. Sailors want to meet them because the song is so beautiful, but they are being lured on to the rocks to their deaths. So Odysseus wants to hear the song so much that he gets all his men to block up their ears with wax. Then he orders them to strap him to the mast and then they're all in the ship and they can't hear anything, but he can and even though he's strapped to the mast he's screaming at his men, shouting at them to release him because he wants to go to these women – even though he knows that will kill him, that he knows the whole idea of the beautiful song is to take him to his destruction.

That perfectly sums up temptation. "Odysseus" means "victim of enmity"... aren't people so often getting in our own way? I know that I was for so many years in so many ways my own worst enemy, and still can be if I don't stay on top of it all.

That's why throughout recovery, tests, temptations and trials are sent every which way: one week it's lust, the next impatience, the week after it's to take a check on pride, intolerance and self-pity. All these character defects have to be removed because otherwise they will hinder and make impossible continued recovery and the duty that will transform the person into a sort of hero who can pass on the joys of recovery to others who are drowning in the dark stormy sea of despair.

Tests, temptations and trials that are put in front of someone are to see how they are doing. Working the 12 Steps means in general you learn how to deal with them, that is then: how to live life on life's terms. You have been given the guidebook for life. You can now "do life" where you once couldn't seem to even figure out how to tie your shoelaces.

Remember we are looking at achieving the purest form of ourselves, when the base metal turns into gold. An astounding connection here is that which we translate as "holy" in the Bible is derived from

Hebrew meaning "to purify". When an addict is drug-free we say they are "clean", as in no longer impure.

Says the Twelve Steps And Twelve Traditions: "We shall need to raise our eyes toward perfection, and be ready to walk in that direction." This isn't to be perfect in a vain sense, like The Fonz thought as he looked in the mirror! The word "perfect" is from Latin perfectus meaning "completed". It's what we aim for, for we surely don't want to miss the mark. Yet some people are so off mark their entire life – despite material gains and status – that it is obvious they cannot even begin to imagine what they're missing.

Hitting the target takes an immense amount of effort, dedication and discipline. Nobody said it would be easy. It's also something innate in us: there is no sense of achievement without achieving something. And we are designed so that we cherish this.

It's like the story of the old painter who painted beautiful pictures and then cut them up before giving them to a group of children. The children loved putting the pieces together, so they could finally see what the old painter's picture was each time. One day the old painter thought he would save the children the time and bother of piecing it together, and so he presented them with the picture complete. He was aghast to see that instead of the smiles he was used to getting at this stage, they all looked disappointed... Or put another way, as a young child would you have ever bothered having a running race with your dad if you knew he was going to just let you win every time?

In any case, if it was easy… then everyone would just gain it and then just as easily throw it away again in the knowing that it was easy to get back. It has to be hard-earned so that it is valued as much as you value life itself. Because without it there is only the going back and the getting worse.

Who on this planet would want to die knowing they hadn't lived to their true potential, that they had not been true to themselves, that in their one chance at this life they had never discovered the real person they were meant to be and lived for their real purpose?

Surely we all want to be complete? We want that victory.

We must be humble at all times. It is said that Bill W wrote his first draft of Step 7 to say: "Humbly, on our knees, asked God to forgive our shortcomings." It is to gain the perspective to see that building our character and spiritual values always have to come above all. Without doing it this way it is often said in the 12 Steps groups that "you will lose whatever you put above your recovery anyway" – which means your family, your relationship, your home, your work, your income, your freedom, and your life. So we need to put it first, and to face what was wrong, heal those scars, and drop all those irritating pebbles and those heavy and dark boulders we insisted on carrying and dragging around with us.

Many people say The Seventh Step Prayer on their knees at the end of their walking through this Step: "My Creator, I am now willing that you should have all of me, good and bad. I pray that you now remove from me every single defect of character which stands in the way of my usefulness to you and my fellows. Grant me strength, as I go out from here, to do your bidding."

In Inferno, Dante goes through Hell right past Satan – who is frozen up to his chest in ice. Satan has no personality, is slobbering and says nothing at all, not a word. Hell is heavy and dark, and totally iced over, the watery chaos having been frozen by the icy wind caused by Satan flapping his six wings. Satan constantly flaps them, attempting to escape from this Hell; but he cannot because he's trapped in the ice. If he stopped flapping, it is expected the ice would melt and Satan would be able to move – but to escape from Hell he'd have to beat his wings again to fly away, which would freeze the water over once more, and so trap Satan there again. This terrifying paradox of his means of escape being the cause of his imprisonment means Satan will be stuck at the bottom of an icy Hell forever, continually entrapping himself by eternally attempting to flee.

It is surely symbolic of how we all so often get in our own way (or our ego plans gets in the way of God's true purpose for us) and we are our own worst enemy, trapping ourselves in a perpetual state of hell on Earth. It's really not supposed to be like this.

Once past Satan and through icy Hell, Dante reaches the Mount of Purgatory – where people get purged, where souls are purified. This mountain has different terraces on which they are made to realise their sin: so this includes the Lustful who have to go through immense fierce walls of flame; the Gluttonous who are starved by trees with fruit that's always out of reach; the Slothful who have to continually run around in ceaseless activity; the Wrathful who are left to walk around in thick acrid smoke, which symbolises the blinding effect of anger; the Envious who have their eyelids stitched shut with wire; and the Proud who are bent over by the weight of huge boulders on their backs, and as they walk around the mountain's terrace they can see attractive sculptures expressing humility. At the summit of the Mount of Purgatory is the Earthly Paradise, representing the beautiful purity that existed before Adam and Eve fell.

The point is that to reach the entity of living in paradise on Earth you cannot skip this going through seeing how you've missed the mark. Then, and only then, can you be rid of your imperfections in order to be pure, and so then relentlessly you as you are meant to be.

8. Be relentlessly fearless

Step 8: Made a list of all persons we had harmed, and became willing to make amends to them all.

At this stage the biggest fear facing the potential hero is fear itself. Fear is everyone's greatest foe… It is like a dark infinite echo chamber inside the mind and soul of humankind.

How then does anyone become fearless? By facing it, with the faith that you can and will face it. It's the only way. Fear knocked at the door; Faith answered, and nobody was there.

But you cannot think yourself fearless. It takes action. Your conscious actions are the outer reflection of your inner transformation. These actions often take courage. And faith, including the belief that you won't get killed. But that your persona, the ego, that which you put out there as a mask for all to see, will be killed. That is a fact if you do take the action that this stage is a preparation towards carrying out.

You have to absolutely believe that whatever power is out there is bigger than you: the Force, a Higher Power, the Creative Intelligence, the Universe, Allah, God… Your ego will die. Lose your life to find it. This is the aim. But you will live. The real you.

Who you're supposed to be. You need to believe this, to know it. Have faith. You'll see it when you believe it.

There can be no resurrection, no rebirth without first dying. It's about reaching nirvana that is the final goal of Buddhism, a transcendent state in which there is neither suffering, desire, nor sense of self – from Sanskrit nirva meaning to "be extinguished".

Known as the St Francis Prayer, this could also apply to the Hero's Journey or completing the 12 Steps.
Lord, make me an instrument of thy peace;
That where there is hatred, I may bring love.
That where there is wrong, I may bring the spirit of forgiveness.
That where there is discord, I may bring harmony.
That where there is error, I may bring truth.
That where there is doubt, I may bring faith.
That where there is despair, I may bring hope.
That where there are shadows, I may bring light.
That where there is sadness, I may bring joy.
Lord, grant that I may seek rather to comfort, than to be comforted.
To understand, than to be understood.
To love, than to be loved.
For it is by self-forgetting that one finds.
It is by forgiving that one is forgiven.
It is by dying that one awakens to Eternal Life.

This is why in the Hero's Journey stories the hero, who we relate to because they have represented us and our own desires and fears, does often appear to physically die. Then we as the audience, after feeling dismayed, are full of utter vitality as we see their return from death. It's like the hero in the story is reborn. They are resurrected.

Just like the Hero's Journey story of Jesus Christ. "I am the resurrection and the life." No one person is going to feel more alive than just after they think they've died. It's an elation!

Step 8 is when you write down a thorough and honest list of all people you have or may have harmed. In AA's Twelve Steps And Twelve Traditions book it says: "To define the word 'harm' in a practical way, we might call it the result of instincts in collision, which cause physical, mental, emotional, or spiritual damage to people."

What in us injured or disturbed other people? Note that Step 8 says the word "all" twice to emphasise that there is no one we should think of missing out. And in the Twelve Steps And Twelve Traditions it puts it strongly too: "We can now commence to ransack memory for the people to whom we have given offence." It goes on to say that we must walk back through our lives "year by year".

If the person wants to get the reward, to gain the treasure, they must put everyone down, from throughout their entire life, all their life, right back to childhood and school days. As far as memory will reach. It does not say anywhere that you can skip out a year here or there, or this person or that just because you don't think you need to go back there, or because you find some ego-driven justification – and the damaged portion of your ego that has always caused you so much trouble will always be looking for excuses like this. As said before, it always will because it wants to continue being your master, to crack the whip on your naked broken back.

So completing Step 8 is another significant step on your way to telling that sick egotistical voice where to go. You need to do this to break free of that bondage. Your Step 4 list will help here for you to write down everyone who you potentially need to make an amend towards. There might be some others not on your Step 4 list, people who you didn't have any resentment towards. You might even include places on your list, a pub or a town in which you caused harm, and your Step 9 amend might be re-visiting that place to behave as a decent person, to do something good there.

Anyone who misses being thorough and honest about this will not get the reward, they are not going to go into the darkest part of the cave, slay the dragon and collect the treasure that is there for them (and it's there for them whether they get it or not, and in fact the dragon doesn't even have any use for it other than it's something to guard…).

Those who omit a period of their life or someone here, by some way justifying it, are not going to get that which they most need. Your sponsor needs to make this known without any doubt. It's why a sponsor is vital in doing the 12 Steps. Do not try this without guidance, do not try this at home alone! You need to be with someone who has trodden where you are heading, who has already faced their greatest fear by making their own amends (face to face whenever possible) to people he or she has harmed.

When someone asks another to sponsor them, the usual question the potential sponsor asks is, while looking at the other person in the eye: "Are you willing to go to any length?" But perhaps the person at this stage of doing the 12 Steps makes it seen that they are not willing to go to any length. They need to be reminded what they agreed at the outset of the 12-Step journey. It's abundantly clear. Deciding who you make your amends to as you will with your sponsor at this stage is nothing to do with you: you don't decide. Trust your mentor's wisdom and knowing.

Or maybe the person is just not ready for this. They have not reached the required courage quite possibly because somewhere in the previous 12 Steps, they've missed something out. They have not been completely thorough and honest. They will know this somewhere deep inside. Then they are not fully prepared for this. They are likely to return to the place from which they were trying to get away from, and mostly that place will swiftly become much worse than it was before.

Anyone who has spent any sort of time in 12 Steps meetings will have heard from those who return to the meetings after slips where they have fallen back into their addiction. Never does anyone say it was okay or it was better than before, but still a bit terrible or that it was actually fine. Without fail, because addiction is a progressive illness, it is very rapidly much worse than where they were when they previously stopped. They frequently say, even if they have for instance been sober for 25 years, that it was straight back to the hell they were in a quarter of a century previously, and then got even worse. Some who slip, are never heard from: they are dead within hours of slipping.

The Twelve Steps And Twelve Traditions covers the "justification" of not taking this Step: "Why, we cried, shouldn't bygones be bygones? Why do we have to think of these people at all? These were some of the ways in which fear conspired with pride to hinder our making a list of all the people we had harmed." It also says in the Twelve Steps And Twelve Traditions: "If we are now about to ask forgiveness for ourselves, why shouldn't we start out by forgiving them, one and all?"

This is a tough task all round. The road to spiritual awakening is broad, but there are certain pass points that everyone must go through. The awakening of the hero inside will not happen otherwise, their treasure never secured.

It follows that way in the Hero's Journey too. In the Hero's Journey, the mentor may come back into the story here. If the mentor was killed earlier, an object they gave is of value or some of their words of wisdom or a memory of their courageous deeds may come back to the potential hero, as happens with Luke in Star Wars when he hears mentor Obi-Wan Kenobi's voice urging him to go with the Force.

In Step 8, there is something else to do that is massively illuminating and humbling. It can frequently be extremely emotional too. That is to go through the list of people you have on your Step 8 and for each one, on a separate piece of paper, write down something that you did that caused them harm. Keep it brief, to a short sentence.

Now next to that, write down how you would have felt if somebody had done that to you. Picture it in your mind's eye. Consider the words carefully that describe how you'd have been at that moment. Really challenge yourself. That is, rather than put down "I'd have been a bit angry", really think about it: ask yourself, wouldn't you have felt perhaps more like enraged, seething, or maybe for a split-second you'd even have felt such malevolence as to be murderous? When you've written all you have to write on this, it is suggested you go through it with your sponsor, who may still challenge you further as to just how far your emotions and reactions might have gone.

As with Step 4 and Step 5 this is in no way to punish yourself, but it is to help you realise that all actions have a consequence, like those ripples on a pond or sometimes like a storm wave crashing in. What we say and do shapes the world around us. Forgive yourself, for you were someone who was not well. All that you are doing now is about getting recovered and then ready to live a new way. The new life is infinitely better. Doing this part of this Step will undoubtedly make you think about the best way to conduct yourself.

All the Steps so far are preparation to give you the strength, belief and courage that is required for this ordeal. If any of the trials and tests before now have not been fully completed and passed, the potential hero will fail.

For now is the real thing. It takes everything you have, and more that you didn't think you could ever have. Remember, if the rewards were that easy to get, everyone would just grab them.

So the preparation needs to have been infinite, for the reward is infinite.

9. Be courageous

Step 9: Made direct amends to such people wherever possible, except when to do so would injure them or others.

This is the entering of the innermost part of the darkest cave to face and slay the dragon that's otherwise going to finish you off – representing someone's greatest fear or fears, or representing fear itself that taints, poisons and destroys lives. Everything – all the Steps so far, every trial, tribulation, temptation and test that has come before – have made the potential hero ready for this moment.

This is the moment when the hero steps forward. This is the key point of the journey. Anyone who is here has gone to any length. They are ultimately prepared. As they have to be. All the previous stages have been moving to this place, all that follows will move out from it.

They are ready to slay the dragon. Deep down, somewhere in the heart and soul, they have known all along, from the moment of the Call To Adventure or the entering the rooms of a 12-Step recovery meeting, that they have to do something like this. That is when the continuation of life as it was before became for the first time more terrifying than going this new way into the unknown. There was the knowing that if they didn't get prepared and face the dragon, then the dragon would come for them and slay them anyway.

And that, they knew, would have been entirely on the dragon's terms. It likely would not have been swift. It usually isn't. The dragon would have enjoyed playing with them, a rip of skin here and there, flames at will to burn flesh, pin its victim down, claw away at the wounds...

You need the qualities of good judgement, a sense of timing, courage, readiness to take the full consequences of your past, and prudence – but always ensure that prudence doesn't mean evasion! Be absolutely sure that you're not delaying because you're afraid. Maintain a steady purpose.

Now the potential hero must confront whatever or whoever holds the ultimate power in their life. In many myths and stories this represents a parental figure: someone or something with an incredible all-consuming power over the potential hero.

"Atonement consists in no more than the abandonment of that self-generated double monster – the dragon thought to be God (superego) and the dragon thought to be Sin (repressed id)," explained Campbell. "But this requires an abandonment of the attachment to ego itself, and that is what is difficult. ... The hero transcends life with its peculiar blind spot and for a moment rises to a glimpse of the source. He beholds the face of the father, understands – and the two are atoned."

In The Empire Strikes Back, Luke discovers that Darth Vader is his father and subsequently escapes by falling into a chute beneath him. In Indiana Jones And The Last Crusade, the hero and his father drink holy water from the Holy Grail, which grants everlasting life.

The 12 Steps are about ego reduction and spiritual growth, two aspects that are on balancing scales meaning that when one is up the other has to go down. The ultimate aim here is for loss of ego, to be rid of the restrictive bondage of self. You need to hold here as the main spirit of what you are doing, as the hero does in the Hero's Journey, is to take responsibility for the well-being of others.

So the potential hero, close now to being a hero, has to summon every bit of what they always knew to be true and slay the dragon. They need to find that something that was always in them.

In Step 9 it means making amends, directly and that means "wherever possible" face to face with anyone you have caused spiritual, physical, emotional or mental harm to, and it means asking for forgiveness in a humble way. Your internal chaos needs to be conquered to become order, to be complete. Atone, at one.

Asking for forgiveness may be worded something like this, that's been used as a guide by many who've previously done their Step 9s: **"My behaviour has been very selfish and arrogant** [or examples of any of the 14 defects of character]. **I've been full of self-pity** [or examples of any of the 14 defects of character] **For example, I...** [give a couple of examples concerning the person you are making the amend to, keeping it brief and in mind that it must not cause them any harm]. **How you have dealt with me is nothing short of amazing. Your patience and understanding has been unbelievable and much better than I could have done. I'm going through the 12 Steps now and as part of my recovery programme I have to make amends for the harm I've done. If I don't I'll start drinking** [or whatever it is] **again. It's not that I'm all of a sudden a great person, it's because I don't want to relapse. I understand if you won't, but please find it in your heart to forgive me. I know I won't be able to make up for what I've done but if I can in any way, please let me know."**

Clearly, this wording needs to be adapted, if for instance you are going to make amends in a shop or business that you once stole from. But remember that the essence of these words has worked for many thousands before you.

This is about facing fear. Being courageous. That could mean a financial debt to pay, where a promise is to pay what you owe, however measly the instalments might be to start with, and a vow to pay as much as you can as and when things improve financially for you. That could mean the police are called, prison is even a possibility, or anger, even a punch. (Naturally, if the anger is too much, of course you can remove yourself from the situation, or if physical aggression is used against you, then using self-defence and calling the police is likely the best option.)

But this is always with guided advice from your sponsor, and most people realise their worst fears never materialise. In fact, the reaction is often quite the opposite to those worst fears.

In the Twelve Steps And Twelve Traditions it says: "Are we going to be so rigidly righteous about making amends that we don't care what happens to the family and home? Or do we first consult those who are to be gravely affected? Do we lay the matter before our sponsor or spiritual adviser, earnestly asking God's help and guidance – meanwhile resolving to do the right thing when it becomes clear, cost what it may? Of course, there is no pat answer which can fit all such dilemmas. But all of them do require a complete willingness to make amends as fast and as far as may be possible in a given set of conditions."

It's important to remember to have a good chat with your sponsor about any amends that might bring harm to your family or yourself. It's for a thorough discussion as to whether an amend is made that might see you losing your income or even your freedom, for instance, that then causes harm to your family. In Step 8 you needed to be willing to write down every single amend that is possibly needed to be made – but talk them all through. You need to stand up and take responsibility here.

But some it will be decided should be left, although there may well be a way of making some sort of amends. (Sometimes a charity might benefit here.) In others, where justifications for not doing them have been imaginatively created, it will be realised with your sponsor's guidance that in fact these amends do need to be made. So you need to make them.

A phone or video-call is not as direct as amends can be – unless there really is no other possible way (there nearly always is, if you are prepared to go to any lengths). Making an amend without facing the person means the potential hero has the option that is the equivalent of running from the cave. Fleeing as soon as the dragon's eyes widen. If it's not an amend made face to face, it's too easy to end the phone call or slam down the laptop lid to stop the video call: basically, you could run or hide. Even if you don't end the call like this, you have not been as courageous as you could be because you know that option of ending the call is there. Face to face is the best way all round.

After your amend is made, it is for you to humbly accept the reaction now, whatever that involves.

Without saying another word. It is not and never simply to go over anything again. It is not to expect an apology from the other person. That's their business. (And you can afterwards write a Step 10 if it bothers you.) It is to clean up your side of the street.

A wonderful thing that most people making their amends in Step 9 soon realise at this point is that other people are generally very forgiving, with many realising that others are much more forgiving than they ever were. It is a significant lesson.

Many start with a few of the less daunting amends to make, to see how it is. They are often greatly encouraged when they start to realise the substantial benefits, and the glowing and frequently euphoric feeling that comes.

However, after a few Step 9 amends, with some people there may also be the temptation to miss out the more dreaded meetings that have still to come, that may seem overwhelming. People at this stage often create seemingly sound and justifiable excuses for missing these. Or they may just delay, saying the time is not right, when really the chance to do this is already there. "Made direct amends." But a hero needs to face the dragon and all it has. Now is the time.

With the 12 Steps, a sponsor's guidance is essential again here because amends are not made if it will cause more harm to others. But see how it doesn't say harm to the person in recovery. You have to be fearless with this.

If not there is no way to carry on living in hell on Earth anyway. The dragon has been ruling for too long, this is the only way of ensuring it doesn't destroy, turn a person into ashes.

Then, having slain the dragon, the treasure is there: the treasure is in fact in slaying the dragon.

This is the point of realisation in which a greater understanding is achieved. Armed with this new knowledge and perception, the hero emerges, perhaps gasping for breath after nearly drowning for so long in the mundane dark waters. But those gasps then become breaths that then become easy breaths. Just like the lotus flower grows in muddy water, until it rises and blooms above the murk to achieve enlightenment. To be what it's supposed to be in its full power, glory and beauty.

This is what the hero went on the journey to get. All the previous steps serve to prepare and complete – to purify – the hero for this step, since in many myths the boon is something transcendent such as the elixir of life. As Campbell put it: "This is the miraculous energy of the thunderbolts of Zeus, Yahweh, and the Supreme Buddha, the fertility of the rain of Viracocha, the virtue announced by the bell rung in the Mass at the consecration, and the light of the ultimate illumination of the saint and sage. Its guardians dare release it only to the duly proven."

In many Hero's Journey stories this moment, when it is released to the duly proven, is often signified with huge splashes of billowing white light, fireworks of the soul, a celebration of the spirit within us all. Look to the explosive endings of most James Bond films: when 007 gets to know that light-filled entity right there inside is Heaven itself.

In the Beginning, God created the light and then afterwards the sun and moon. That light has been right inside you all along. It's how we're made, all of us with this remarkable human condition.

Or as Dorothy puts it at the end of The Wizard Of Oz: "If I ever go looking for my heart's desire again, I won't look any further than my own backyard."

10. Keep growing, and say sorry when you make a mistake

Step 10: Continued to take personal inventory, and when we were wrong, promptly admitted it.

This is the start of the road back to the ordinary world. But that world will never again be grey and drab as it was before the journey commenced. There has been a profound change, not in the ordinary world but in the hero's perception of it all.

Everything looks the same, but everything is different.

So while Steps 4, 5, 8 and 9 dealt with historical matters, this is where you start to carry that same principle into everyday life, in the now. One day at a time – and just for today.

It's suggested you vow now to keep on growing by keeping on looking honestly at yourself, at where you could have done things differently and how to keep making progress towards being the most complete person you can be, the best ideal, with a genuine gratitude for what there is about you. Now the past is settled, the challenges of the present can be faced.

The real world has to be lived in once again. In AA literature the 12 Steps are described as "a bridge to normal living". This is where the bridge is crossed. But seeing the world for the miracle it is has become the new normal. Says AA's Daily Reflections book: "Each day brings new experience, awareness, greater hope, deeper faith, broader tolerance. I must maintain these attributes or I will have nothing to pass on."

Those who've previously walked along the spiritual path know that nobody can make much of life until self-searching becomes a daily routine. If not done with every fibre – fearlessly, honestly and thoroughly – and if not then maintained with discipline, then the dragon's ghost will return to haunt and come back to life and conquer once more and finally kill.

It is to trust that this world is a loving world. It is to know that we are all here through love, created and given the gift of life, breath, a heartbeat, by the Creative Intelligence that loves us and has an amazing purpose for each and every one of us. We are born through our parents but not of them. That absolute love that made us this way is what we aim for with humble hearts.

If need be, in life, there is a need to swiftly ask for forgiveness, not only to others but to ourselves – and to the greater power whatever that is with which you now have a relationship. Just trust. For it is a journey from Hell to Heaven. There's no need to go

221

back, but as with all things for humans, it depends on a daily maintenance. If this is neglected, just as with someone who gets physically fit by going to the gym every day for six months, it will waste away if we stop doing what we've been doing.

So we continue doing the three-column lists as we did in Step 4. It might seem like a lot of writing at first, but this is like revision for the soul. Each time we get a resentment (and there's no need for secrets now you have your trusted guide/sponsor/mentor/spiritual coach) – it needs to be written down. We learn more about what makes us tick each time we do. At first, starting Step 10 at the same time as Step 4, there might be lots of things that have to be written down, lots of things during the day where we feel our feelings rising, usually uncomfortable ones, although we must also remember to write down if we have self-congratulatory feelings when we achieve something, so that we keep such as arrogance in check. We must then always give thanks to the greater power for any of these achievements. Spiritually awoken people also give thanks for the seemingly bad things too as they are a chance to learn and grow some more.

At some stage, often within weeks of starting to write down Step 10s, something will happen that we realise would have usually caused a resentment, perhaps a major one, and yet because of our new awareness of ourselves and our inner activities it does not cause anything to stir in us. Consequently it doesn't need to be written down. We are beginning to comprehend the word serenity.

It requires hard and diligent work, especially at the beginning, and we must also be disciplined to maintain it. (That word "discipline", originally detested by so many who are reminded of strict parents and schools, is in fact from Latin disciplina meaning "instruction, knowledge" as in the word "disciple". It's good to know.) It has to be tough work like this or we might get complacent. It has to be something that needs to be worked at, or it could just be gained by everyone at a click of the fingers. Then dropped and regained at another click of the fingers. It needs to be something that's worked at so that it becomes valued and protected, as valued as life itself, for that really is what it is.

However, having found bliss and enlightenment as well as excitement in the other world, the hero may not actually want to return to the ordinary world. "The full round, the norm of the monomyth, requires that the hero shall now begin the labour of bringing the runes of wisdom, the Golden Fleece, or his sleeping princess, back into the kingdom of humanity, where the boon may redound to the renewing of the community, the nation, the planet or the ten thousand worlds," Campbell said. "But the responsibility has been frequently refused. Even Gautama Buddha, after his triumph, doubted whether the message of realization could be communicated, and saints are reported to have died while in the supernal ecstasy."

Frodo is so exhausted in The Lord Of The Rings after destroying the ring that he simply wants to give up and die rather than make the return journey. So, like this, the return to the normal world may be resisted, in the beginning... But when the hero – for now they have found that hero inside, that is inside all of us, waiting to burst out like when Superman rips open his shirt to reveal what's there underneath: now they are a hero. And a hero realises they can take back what they have gained – the "boon" – and share it. They realise this is their duty. The Adventure called them for this. When they know this is what they have do, to keep living by spirit over ego, any resistance goes away.

In fact, it needs to be given away to keep it. It is part of the process of progress towards perfection, completeness. So the hero at this stage again crosses the threshold between the two worlds, returning to the ordinary world with that which they have gained. They will now use that for the benefit of others and the world around them. The hero has been transformed and has gained new wisdom and spiritual power over both worlds.

It's the gift of giving. Who knew this was the way to fill up the inner emptiness, the hell inside, the drab life with no meaning or purpose, and shine over what you once thought was a forever darkness with the infinite light...

11. Meditate as soon as you wake up

Step 11: Sought through prayer and meditation to improve our conscious contact with God as we understood Him, praying only for knowledge of His will for us and the power to carry that out.

Hero's journeys happen more than once, so long as we are open to them.

"What I think is that a good life is one hero journey after another," said Campbell. "Over and over ... There's always the possibility of a fiasco. But there's also the possibility of bliss."

Step 11 is the resolution, when you resolve to carry on walking along this golden path of the new way. As has been said before, there can be no resurrection without crucifixion... Life crucifies all of us, to differing extents. We live in a world, certainly in the West, that tells us it shouldn't be like this, that life should always be a bed of roses, with no thorns and no pain or suffering. But there is, and it's all part of the design for human life: through the pain, we should gain. It's always a signpost pointing to where we need to head for new growth, to realise our full potential. It's the resistance that's always the real problem. That can take the form of addictions or other things that numb us, consume us or mask over what we really need to be paying attention to and taking action on.

So the hero emerges from the extraordinary world, totally transformed by their experience, resurrected into a new being by the experience. What they find was always inside, but they needed to go through what they did to discover it, to release it and then know it.

You could say that as we're created in the image of God, we're all little Gods. The rebirth has taken place, the key to life has been discovered. God is within, but we must always know that we are not God.

In recovery, this discovery, this new fearlessness, it must be maintained by growth and that means we must get to know the Higher Power that gave us our first breath, that granted us this life and light inside all along from our beginning. We do that by developing our relationship with whatever we have come to know is the greater power that has always been guiding us. We can do that in exactly the same way we develop any relationship: by spending time together and getting to know each other. This is achieved through daily prayer and meditation, ideally first thing in the stillness of the morning.

In stillness (and silence) seems to work best for most people. It's the most energising way to wake up, otherwise it's the picking up of a phone to scroll through lots of bombarding information, often that gives rise to such as pride, self-pity, intolerance, envy and so on. Already energy is being used up. Or other people wake up and rush in to everything they think they have to do that day. It's not a healthy start.

So, prayer means "to ask", and many people say meditation is when we observe and listen, including of ourselves. The experience of prayer and meditation across the centuries is colossal. It could be considered arrogant of anyone to dismiss it (particularly prior to investigation: the greatest form of ignorance), for they are dismissing tens of thousands of years of human experience, understanding and knowledge. As well as every morning, it's suggested to finish each day with prayer and meditation.

In the Twelve Steps And Twelve Traditions this dismissing of these two vital assets for humans is addressed: "We recoiled from meditation and prayer as obstinately as the scientist who refused to perform a certain experiment lest it prove his pet theory wrong. Of course we finally did experiment, and when unexpected results followed, we felt different; in fact we knew different; and so we were sold on meditation and prayer. And that, we have found, can happen to anybody who tries. … Those of us who have come to make regular use of prayer would no more do without it than we would refuse air, food or sunshine. And for the same reason. When we refuse air, light or food the body suffers. And when we turn away from meditation and prayer, we likewise deprive our minds, our emotions and our intuitions of vitally needed support. As the body can fail its purpose for lack of nourishment, so can the soul."

With the right attitude, it works for anybody. Millions of people have discovered this. So prayer and meditation for 30 minutes, no less, every morning on waking up. It can include a mental gratitude list, it can include listening to your breathing and feeling your heartbeat. It can include listening to the birdsong and looking to the horizon, or it can just as much be about listening for the silence from which all the inner-city noise comes and watching the stillness of the urban plane tree.

It can be like having a relaxed chat with the best friend ever, the greatest parent, the one who always has time to really listen to you, to all your worries and aims, the one who knows you matter and just how very much. Or it may work for you to speak with the one who always existed, that did not begin to exist, which did not come into being. And then listen and look and feel, even smell and taste, for the answers. Your gut may well help more than your brain here.

It could include the Lord's Prayer, or the previously mention Serenity Prayer and St Francis Prayer. In doing Step 11 every day, it is suggested that you pray for knowledge of your Higher Power's will "and the power to carry that out". Raise your heart and mind. Ask for the grace to bring love, forgiveness, harmony, truth, faith, hope, light and joy to every person. That will certainly do no harm.

Prayer and meditation can be whatever works best for you. But it needs to be done, for in the doing there is already gain.

In the book Alcoholics Anonymous it says: "We realise we know only a little. God will constantly disclose more to you and to us. Ask Him in your morning meditation what you can do each day for the man who is still sick. The answers will come, if your own house is in order. But obviously you cannot transmit something you haven't got. See to it that your relationship with Him is right, and great events will come to pass for you and countless others. This is the Great Fact for us."

Search not for your ego's plan for yourself any longer but for your spirit's purpose for you. This will bring together what the psychiatrist M Scott Peck was saying when he spoke about the need with his clients who were suffering to unite their conscious with their unconscious: "It is because our conscious self resists our unconscious wisdom that we become ill."

While prayer and meditation is the way to start every day, it can be for any part of the day too. As well as again in the evening before going to sleep, it's especially useful at any time if you feel choked up with such as fear, frustration, anger, cannot understand something or need guidance in making a decision.

Those who get in the daily routine of prayer and meditation develop a wisdom beyond. It will become something as regular as cleaning your teeth and having a shower, and soon if a meditation is missed you will be reminded by yourself that you've missed it.

The 1990's song Search For The Hero by M People sums this all up so well:
"Just seek yourself and you will shine.
You've got to search for the hero inside yourself,
Search for the secrets you hide.
Search for the hero inside yourself
Until you find the key to your life.
In this life, long and hard though it may seem,
Live it as you'd live a dream.
Aim so high. Just keep the flame of truth burning bright.
The missing treasure you must find
Because you and only you alone
Can build a bridge across the stream."

Now the hero inside has been found, it must be kept. This world needs you.

12. Remember everyone's name, be kind

Step 12: Having had a spiritual awakening as the result of these steps, we tried to carry this message to alcoholics, and to practice these principles in all our affairs.

It says "alcoholics" in this original Step 12 wording as written by Bill W for AA, but in other 12 Steps groups this word is replaced with the particular addiction, be it "addicts", "compulsive overeaters", "gamblers" or "sex and love addicts". In Al-Anon it simply says: "Having had a spiritual awakening as the result of these steps, we tried to carry this message to others, and to practice these principles in all our affairs." In Emotions Anonymous it simply says: "... we tried to carry this message...". It can be this, to anyone who it can help, that is to everyone. Remember that such as alcoholism and other addictions are different symptoms of the same mental health problems that most frequently have started with a spiritual sickness.

Now the hero has returned to the ordinary world "as the result of these steps" with their treasure and the wonderful energy it releases has been awoken. They have been to where they least wanted to go and consequently they have found what they most needed.

It is that which was always inside them. That is love, light, fearlessness, infinite belief, faith and hope – all of these. A new force of supernatural strength.

It means that now you will have enough courage to leave that relationship, to quit that job, to make that move... Unless you're in danger there's no need to rush at these things, but know that now you can. And know that – so long as they fit with your new spiritually awoke way of living – you can now reach every single one of your dreams.

There is a wonderful spiritual paradox: it gives a freedom from the fear of dying, which is the freedom to live. As Mitch Albom wrote in Tuesdays With Morrie, the voice of his dying friend, his teacher, Morrie Schwartz: "The truth is, once you learn how to die, you learn how to live."

Morrie also said: "Giving is living" and "The way you get meaning into your life is to devote yourself to loving others, devote yourself to your community around you, and devote yourself to creating something that gives you purpose and meaning." That's what Step 12 is about.

The hero has become comfortable and competent in both the inner and outer worlds now. Instincts have been restored to their true purpose. Giving away to others what has been given must now be humbly presented. Twelve Steps literature suggests "attraction not promotion". Create your own corner.

Look after yourself. Eat well. Regularly exercise your mind and body. Remember people's name. Be kind. Show love. That includes to yourself for you must care for yourself as someone who really matters, for you do matter – as you always have, as does everyone ever who's been given the gift of life. You are here for an amazing reason! Your Higher Power is crazy for you! You were not saved from drowning only to be battered on the beach.

You need to give constantly without expectation of any repayment. It is unconditional and universal love in action. Absolute Love. There comes the realisation that everyone is in everyone – everyone is actually one.

Aldous Huxley wrote in The Doors Of Perception: "The man who comes back through the Door in the Wall will never be quite the same as the man who went out. He will be wiser but less sure, happier but less self-satisfied, humbler in acknowledging his ignorance yet better equipped to understand the relationship of words to things, of systematic reasoning to the unfathomable mystery which it tries, forever vainly, to comprehend."

The hero must always be careful with the treasure here. Be grateful for this blessing at all times. Always be humble.

Joseph Campbell wrote in The Hero With A Thousand Faces: "The individual, through prolonged psychological disciplines, gives up completely all attachment to his personal limitations, idiosyncrasies, hopes and fears, no longer resists the self-annihilation that is prerequisite to rebirth in the realization of truth, and so becomes ripe, at last, for the great at-one-ment. His personal ambitions being totally dissolved, he no longer tries to live but willingly relaxes to whatever may come to pass in him; he becomes, that is to say, an anonymity."

It's a reason anonymity is so important in 12 Steps recovery, which is why the names of the 12 Steps groups state it so boldly. It's about ego reduction – or even better ego destruction! It's the spiritual solid rock upon which new lives are built. It has been found over the years that many of those who go publicly stating how well they have done in such as achieving sobriety often relapse. It must be remembered that alone, without the help of a greater power, be that thought of as the group or God, anyone who arrives at a 12-Step meeting had failed to beat their addiction doing it their way. Usually repeatedly for many years.

AA co-founder Bill W stated about humility that it was: "The clear recognition of what and who we really are, followed by a sincere attempt to be what we can be." What one can be, one must be.

Clark Kent is a regular guy until Superman is needed. From the Bhagavad Gita it is said: "Be fearless and pure; never waiver in your determination or your dedication to the spiritual life.

Give freely. Be self-controlled, sincere, truthful, loving, and full of the desire to serve."

The hero may well slip back if they don't at least keep trying to give away what they have gained. As CS Lewis put it: "Humility is not thinking less of yourself, it's thinking of yourself less." A humble person makes a greater mentor because they will be steady, patient, open-minded and self-controlled. All of this, again, has to be shared to keep it; it's not just for the hero.

So the hero has their treasure and they need to say to others who come calling for help: "I have my treasure, it is absolutely awesome, it sparkles in every aspect of my life, it is what it's all about: you may be a millionaire but that is mere crumbs compared to all of this." Then they add, fixing the other person or people in their look, the treasure's sparkle reflected in their eyes: "I know how you can get your treasure too. It's there waiting for you. It is only your treasure. Especially for you. Whether you get it or not, it will still be there. It is always there. But only you can get it, and here's how…"

This is Step 12. The sharing that goes on at 12-Step meetings, when someone in recovery talks aloud to the group for a few minutes about, as described in the AA literature, their "experience, strength and hope" is "to carry this message".

Step 12 states confidently: "Having had a spiritual awakening as the result of these steps…". Note that it doesn't say you might get a slight inkling, or you may get a spiritual tingling going on. It emphatically states "a spiritual awakening" and the reason is that if you do the 12 Steps thoroughly, honestly and fearlessly, if you have gone to any length, you will get this result. It is the law.

It is even scientifically proven if science is what you need for proof, because the experiment has been made within 12 Steps groups for decades now and the conclusion of that experiment has to be that if these 12 Steps are walked through as suggested: there will be a spiritual awakening. The word "science" comes from Latin scire meaning "know". So this we know. The 12 Steps work if you work them. It is scientific fact. It is how we humans are made that this will happen as surely as if we never ate we would starve and then die.

But there is the absolute need to continue going to any length, "to practice these principles in all our affairs". In the Hero's Journey, we know the hero has gained something extraordinary now. We know the superhero has their superhero costume on underneath, ready for when needed, to show they are fearless, there for when everyone else is frozen in fear. But although they are transformed, as with anything in the human condition if it is not used it may be lost.

In the 12 Steps, this is one of the other great reasons for the group meetings. It's somewhere someone who's suffering – at rock bottom in hell, the abyss spread all around – can go to as a safe place to look to others who've been where they are who are now out of that hell and who have transformed. The suffering person can see and hear these people. They first gain hope. That hope replaces their hopelessness. Some light shines in the dark. Gradually, if they continue with the 12 Steps, both the hope and the light will grow.

Then this person will be at the turning point, where they too realise they can cross the threshold from the ordinary world that's killing them by the way they are living and enter the extraordinary world that will save them, and in doing so a transformation will happen.

But if they do take the 12 Steps on this same Hero's Journey, then they must become another one who carries the message, who says: "I know how you can get your treasure too. It's there waiting for you. It is only your treasure. Especially for you. Whether you get it or not, it will still be there. It is always there. But only you can get it, and here's how…"

It has gone full circle.

The Twelve Steps And Twelve Traditions says: "When a man or a woman has a spiritual awakening, the most important meaning of it is that he has now become able to do, feel, and believe that which he could not do before on his unaided strength and resources alone. He has been granted a gift which amounts to a new state of consciousness and being. ... What he has received is a free gift, and yet usually, at least in some small part, he has made himself ready to receive it." Those who do the 12 Steps will slip back if they do not help others. So they go from being the sponsee to the sponsor, the student to the teacher, the mentored to the mentor.

Think of Jesus. Muhammad. Buddha.

It is the realisation of the divinity within. Once through Hell, Dante reaches Heaven and everything is light, weightless and bright. People talk of other's achievements not their own. He sees God's face and it is pure love. It is: "the love that moves the sun and the other stars."

Joseph Campbell put it. "Those who know, not only that the Everlasting lives in them, but that what they, and all things, really are is the Everlasting, dwell in the groves of the wish-fulfilling trees, drink the brew of immortality..."

Or as Alcoholics Anonymous says: "We have found much of heaven and we have been rocketed into a fourth dimension of existence of which we had not even dreamed."

In modern culture think of Obi-Wan Kenobi, Morpheus, Dumbledore, Mr Han, Mickey Goldmill, John Keating, Gandalf, Yoda, Carl Conrad Coreander...

"It's an energy field created by all living things. It surrounds us and penetrates us."

"What are you waiting for? You're faster than this. Don't think you are, know you are."

"Soon we must all face the choice between what is right and what is easy."

"Your focus needs more focus."

"You're gonna eat lightning."

"Did they wait until it was too late to make from their lives even one iota of what they were capable?"

"All we have to decide is what to do with the time that is given us."

"Pass on what you have learned."

"And there are just a few who go to Fantastica and come back. And they make both worlds well again."

So when it is gained it must be given away to keep it. That's the never-ending story. Remember, just how this one began, with my son's words.

"It was really scary... but then it was beautiful."

Some Hero's Journey books, films & people

Jesus
Muhammad
Buddha
Moses
ET
Jaws
Alien
Shrek
Rocky
Avatar
Aladdin
The Way
Hercules
Star Trek
Toy Story
Star Wars
Fight Club
The Matrix
Pinocchio
Moby Dick
King Arthur
The Croods
Harry Potter
James Bond
Stand By Me
The Lion King
Jack Reacher
Finding Nemo
Sleeping Beauty
Watership Down
Apocalypse Now
The Wizard Of Oz
Sherlock Holmes
The Hunger Games
Alice In Wonderland
The Lord Of The Rings
The Neverending Story
Shawshank Redemption
St George & the dragon
The Empire Strikes Back
How To Train Your Dragon
The Silence Of The Lambs
Close Encounters Of The Third Kind
Superman, Batman, Spider-Man, Wonder Woman & all superhero films.

The 12 Steps

1: We admitted we were powerless over alcohol – that our lives had become unmanageable.

2: Came to believe that a Power greater than ourselves could restore us to sanity.

3: Made a decision to turn our will and our lives over to the care of God as we understood Him.

4: Made a searching and fearless moral inventory of ourselves.

5: Admitted to God, to ourselves and to another human being the exact nature of our wrongs.

6: Were entirely ready to have God remove all these defects of character.

7: Humbly asked Him to remove our shortcomings.

8: Made a list of all persons we had harmed, and became willing to make amends to them all.

9: Made direct amends to such people wherever possible, except when to do so would injure them or others.

10: Continued to take personal inventory and when we were wrong promptly admitted it.

11: Sought through prayer and meditation to improve our conscious contact with God as we understood Him, praying only for knowledge of His will for us and the power to carry that out.

12: Having had a spiritual awakening as the result of these steps, we tried to carry this message to alcoholics and to practice these principles in all our affairs.